MAGIC, FORM, AND FANTASY · ANCIENT WORLD · MIDDLE
AGES · RENAISSANCE · BAROQUE · MODERN WORLD

STUDY GUIDE

Paul Enea
Art Department
Delaware County C.C.

A HISTORY OF

ART

PAINTING · SCULPTURE · ARCHITECTURE

THIRD EDITION

FREDERICK HARTT
Paul Goodloe McIntire Professor Emeritus of the History of Art, University of Virginia

PRENTICE-HALL, INC.   *and*   HARRY N. ABRAMS, INC.
Englewood Cliffs, New Jersey   New York

Editorial/production supervision and
   interior design: Jacqueline Vernaglia
Manufacturing buyer: Ray Keating

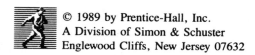 © 1989 by Prentice-Hall, Inc.
A Division of Simon & Schuster
Englewood Cliffs, New Jersey 07632

Printed in the United States of America

10   9   8   7   6   5   4   3   2   1

0-13-049487-9

Prentice-Hall International (UK) Limited, *London*
Prentice-Hall of Australia Pty. Limited, *Sydney*
Prentice-Hall Canada Inc., *Toronto*
Prentice-Hall Hispanoamericana, S.A., *Mexico*
Prentice-Hall of India Private Limited, *New Delhi*
Prentice-Hall of Japan, Inc., *Tokyo*
Simon & Schuster Asia Pte. Ltd., *Singapore*
Editora Prentice-Hall do Brasil, Ltda., *Rio de Janeiro*

CONTENTS

PART TWO

THE ANCIENT WORLD

CHAPTER ONE

CHAPTER TWO

CHAPTER THREE

CHAPTER FOUR

CHAPTER FIVE

CHAPTER SIX

PART THREE

THE MIDDLE AGES

PART FOUR

THE RENAISSANCE

PART FIVE

THE BAROQUE

CHAPTER ONE

CHAPTER TWO

CHAPTER THREE

CHAPTER FOUR

PART SIX

THE MODERN WORLD

CHAPTER ONE

CHAPTER TWO

CHAPTER THREE

CHAPTER FOUR

CHAPTER FIVE

CHAPTER SIX

CHAPTER SEVEN

CHAPTER EIGHT

CHAPTER NINE

CHAPTER TEN

PREFACE

Art is a language which, in all its manifestations, speaks eloquently to the receptive soul. Like all languages, it changes constantly to express the particular customs, ideas, dreams, and appearances of the ever-changing epochs. And, like all languages, it must be learned step by step until it is fully acquired. This work is a manual of instructions to help the student acquire the splendid language of art.

This manual has been conceived as a study guide to accompany Frederick Hartt's *Art: A History of Painting, Sculpture, and Architecture.* It has been carefully constructed to emphasize the significant concepts which Dr. Hartt presents in his text. By means of chronologies, identifications, definitions, discussion questions, matching and comparison sets, geographical locations, and numerous glossaries, this study guide serves to direct the student to the understanding and mastery of art as it has manifested itself throughout the ages.

It is hoped that the assiduous use of this guide in conjunction with Dr. Hartt's text will lead the attentive student to a deeper appreciation of the artistic patrimony of mankind.

Paul J. Enea

INTRODUCTION

1. In your own words, what is your perception of art?

2. The philosopher John Dewey implied that art was an experience. Explain what he meant by this.

3. What do you think is the purpose of art?

4. Until the 19th century, there was a scarcity of women artists. Why?

5. Reality is a perception. Explain this by examining and describing the different perceptions of landscapes in figures 1, 2, 3, 4, and 5.

6. Define the following terms as they relate to the beauty of art:

Form

Line

Light and shade

Color

Space

Pattern

Composition

7. Define *iconography* and state its purpose in art.

8. What is the history of art as you perceive it to be?

9. A total work of art consists of four factors: purpose, style, iconography, and historical position. Explain.

PART ONE

Magic, Form, and Fantasy

CHAPTER ONE

Art Before Writing

1. What is the meaning of and difference between the words *primitive* and *prehistoric*?

2. How do magic, form, and fantasy play a part in the creation of an object of art?

3. Paleolithic art (figs. 14–16) served what religious and instructional purposes?

4. The first statues of human beings and animals served what purpose?

5. Why are the bodies of many female figures (figs. 14 and 15) exaggerated in their proportions?

6. What do the cave paintings in France (figs. 17, 22), Spain (figs. 20, 25), and Sicily (fig. 26) tell us about society in the Paleolithic Age?

7. Describe the most interesting series of plastered skull heads (fig. 28) found in Jericho.

8. What was found at Çatal Hüyük in central Turkey that is important to the history of art?

9. What characterizes megalithic architecture? What was its most likely meaning or function?

PART ONE

Study the *Time Line I* and complete the chart below citing the significant art works of each period.

	Painting	Sculpture	Architecture
Paleolithic (dates:)			
Mesolithic (dates:)			
Neolithic (dates:)			

CHAPTER TWO

The Art Of Later Ethnic Groups

1. During the last half-century, non-European art has come to be held in high respect by Western critics and artists. Explain why.

2. In what ways are non-European artistic traditions similar to European?

3. What was the purpose of African sculpture? What are its characteristics as revealed in the royal *Head of Queen Olokun* (fig. 39)?

4. Much of our knowledge of Benin culture comes from what source?

5. Describe the face and headdress of the serene girl known as the *Princess* (fig. 40).

6. What makes the bronze and wood sculptures in figures 42 and 43 highly sophisticated in style?

7. As a whole, what does the mortuary figure (fig. 44) represent? Describe the abstract characteristics of this work. What does the rhomboid at the base represent according to some authorities?

8. Explain the meaning and purpose of African tribal masks.

9. What characterizes the massive wood carvings of the Yorubas? Use terms such as *vivacity* and *realism* in your discussion.

10. What characterizes Oceanic art as exemplified in the War Shield in figure 48? Use terms such as *abstract*, *curves*, and *ovals* in your discussion.

11. Why is the "Soul Boat" (fig. 49) unique? What was its purpose? Describe it.

12. What conclusions can you draw about the enormous stone figures (fig. 50) on Easter Island?

13. What was the presumed purpose of earth mounds? What makes them aesthetically pleasing to view (fig. 51)?

14. American Indian pipes are brilliantly naturalistic in workmanship. With this statement in mind, explain the meaning and beauty of the Hopewell pipe in figure 52.

15. How are the houses of the Indians of the Southwest (fig. 53) similar in construction to the Çatal Hüyük houses in Turkey (fig. 29)?

16. In what ways are Indian sand paintings similar to the "Action Painters" of the 1950's?

17. Describe the elaborate painted carved bear mask in figure 57.

18. Explain in detail how the art of the Aztecs was intimately related to their religion.

19. On what scale was the architecture of Teotihuacán built? How is it similar to Mesopotamian ziggurats (figs. 123, 125)?

20. What impression was created as one ascended the central staircase of a Mayan pyramid?

21. Describe and state the function of the sculptured Mayan work known as the *Water Goddess* (fig. 63).

22. Describe the scene taking place in the lintel relief in figure 64.

23. The paintings of the Mayas were not limited to religious subjects. Explain this by describing the subject matter in figure 65.

24. Describe the zoomorphic form in the Andean carving in figure 66.

25. Explain why the so-called Gateway of the Sun (fig. 67) "is such a majestic creation."

On the map indicate, by number, the approximate location of the following sites:

1. Conakry	**2.** Abidjan	**3.** Accra
4. Libreville	**5.** Benin	**6.** Ife
7. Ikerre		

MAP 2. WEST AFRICA

PART ONE / Magic, Form, and Fantasy

Associate the location with the work of art by placing its number in the blank provided.

_____ *Bison*	**1.** Chichén Itzá
_____ *Chamois*	**2.** Addaura, Sicily
_____ *Plastered Skull*	**3.** Benin, Nigeria
_____ *Goddess Giving Birth*	**4.** Jericho
_____ Stonehenge	**5.** Çatal Hüyük
_____ *Head of Queen Olokun*	**6.** Salisbury, England
_____ *Leopard*	**7.** Le Mas d'Azil, France
_____ Bakota Guardian	**8.** Altamira, Spain
_____ Simo mask of Nimba	**9.** Guinea Coast
_____ "Soul boat"	**10.** Easter Island
_____ Stone Images	**11.** Ife, Nigeria
_____ The Great Serpent	**12.** New Ireland, New Guinea
_____ Bear Mask	**13.** Ohio
_____ *Water Goddess*	**14.** Gabon, West Africa
_____ *Siege Operations During a Battle*	**15.** Northwest Coast of America
_____ *Raimondi*	**16.** Teotihuacán, Mexico
_____ *Ritual Dance*	**17.** Ancash, Peru

On the map indicate, by number, the approximate location of the following sites:

1. Teotihuacán
4. Managua
7. Lima

2. Tenochitlán
5. Bogotá
8. Machu Picchu

3. Yaxchilán
6. Quito

MAP 4. CENTRAL AND
NORTHWESTERN SOUTH AMERICA

13

PART TWO

The Ancient World

CHAPTER ONE

Egyptian Art

1. In the 5th century B.C., the Greek historian Herodotus wrote that Egypt had "... more wonders than all the world beside ...." What did Herodotus mean by this statement?

2. Summarize the theme of Egyptian art as it relates to immortality.

3. Discuss the significance of the Rosetta stone for Egyptian history and art.

4. List the different periods of Egyptian history.

5. Explain the meaning of Egyptian sculpture in terms of its religion, history, and the pharaoh.

6. Why is the relief structure of the *Palette of King Narmer* (fig. 71) important as an historical and artistic object of art? Describe the conquering king and how he is treating his enemies.

7. In figure 72 of the reverse side of the Palette, describe the appearance of the triumphal king, the ten bodies, and the symbolic meaning of the two-necked panthers.

8. What was the purpose of building pyramids in relation to Egyptian love for life?

9. What material was used to build the *Step Pyramid*? What is the symbolic meaning of the sun's constant rays on these enormous steps?

10. What structural elements are contained in the columns used by the architect Imhotep to support the Entrance Hall at Saqqara (figs. 77 and 78)?

11. How did the limestone statue of *King Zoser* become the prototype for future works?

12. Describe the significance of hands and feet done in profile. Use *Hesira* (fig. 81) as an example.

13. Compare and contrast the "step" pyramid with the "true" pyramid at Giza (fig. 82).

14. For what purpose was the Pyramid of Cheops built? Describe the height, base, acreage, amount of stone, and number of men needed to build it.

15. Why is the Pyramid of Cheops a marvel of daunting engineering monumentality?

16. The word *sphinx* is derived from a Greek verb meaning "to bind together." Use this word to describe the *composite* recumbent sculpture in figure 86.

17. Describe the perfectly preserved black diorite statue of King Chephren (fig. 9) and how it contains many of the canons of Egyptian art.

18. Discuss the symbolic meaning of Cephren being portrayed as "part" of the throne seat. What is the symbolic meaning of the hawk god Horus, perched on the neck of the king?

19. Explain the individuality of each figure in *King Mycerinus Between Two Goddesses* (fig. 87). How is a sense of natural realism and affection created in this work?

20. Compare and contrast the above sculpture with figure 88, *Prince Rabotep and His Wife Nofret*.

21. Explain how the bureaucratic figure known as the *Seated Scribe* is naturalistic and realistic. What characteristics of Egyptian sculpture are contained in this work?

22. How was a symmetrically proportional relief sculpture made, as exemplified in figure 94?

23. Describe how figures 92, 93, 95, and 96 deal with everyday life in Egypt.

24. What makes the Funerary Temple of Mentuhotep (fig. 98) appear to be built on a more "human" scale as compared to earlier Egyptian temples?

25. Compare the brooding King Sesostris III (fig. 99) with the exquisite Princess Sennuwy (fig. 100). Compare the latter with the limestone figure (fig. 101) of Queen Hatshepsut.

26. Describe the kinds of vegetation that were planted at *The Mortuary Temple of Queen Hatshepsut.*

27. Why are the *Temple of Luxor* and *Karnak* wonders of the ancient world? Include in your discussion the massive forest of columns.

28. In what ways were the Egyptian temples (fig. 106) different from Greek temples but similar to Roman ones?

29. Describe the different artistic styles of papyriform columns (figs. 107 and 109) and their symbolic meaning.

30. Describe the *Banquet Scene* in figure 111, *The Blind Harper* (fig. 112), the wall paintings from the Tomb of Sennedjem (fig. 113), and the *Nehamun Hunting Birds* (fig. 114). Include in your discussion the state, movement, attitude, gesture, and symbolic meanings of some of the characters.

31. Explain how naturalism and realism, the maternal and paternal, are portrayed in *King Akhenaten* (fig. 115).

32. The statue of Nefertiti (fig. 117) truly reflects the meaning of her name, "the beautiful one has come." Describe the epitome of feminine beauty in this sculpture.

33. Describe the remote and idealized funeral mask of Tutankhamen and compare it with the relief of him on the back of his wooden throne (fig. 119).

34. Why is the Temple of Abu Simbel so impersonal and inhuman to view?

35. Write an art essay interpreting the following prayer of Ramses III, upon his accession to the throne:

O Gods! I am your son, fashioned by your hands,
Within your golden houses I have worked for you
with gold and silver, turquoise and lapis lazuli.
For you I built castles, sanctuaries, cities,
in which your names are carved for all eternity!

On the map indicate, by number, the approximate location of the following sites:

1. Giza	2. Thebes	3. Karnak
4. Luxor	5. Hierakonpolis	6. Jerusalem
7. Damascus	8. Ashur	9. Dur Sharrukin
10. Baghdad	11. Isin	12. Uruk
13. Ur	14. Babylon	15. Susa

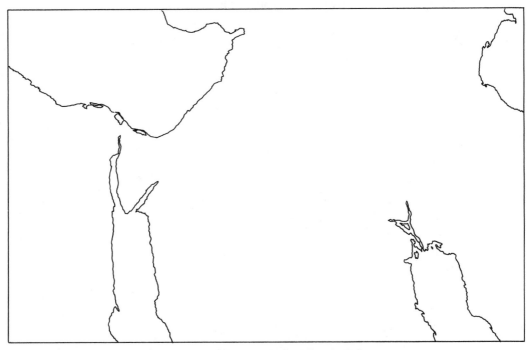

MAP 5. EGYPT AND THE NEAR EAST IN ANCIENT TIMES

PART TWO/Egyptian Art

Prepare a GLOSSARY from the list below by citing one name for each statement.

GLOSSARY

Ankh / Osiris / Ra (Re) / Ramses II / Seti / Sphinx / Tutankhamen / Tuthmosis III / Zoser / Obelisk / Nefertiti / Narmer / Mycerinus / Imhotep / Herodotus / Horus / Chephren / Hatshepsut / Carter / Anubis / Amun / Amenhotep IV

_____ He introduced monotheism into Egyptian religion; attempted to change the artistic life of Egypt by making it more natural and realistic.

_____ Was the deity of Thebes. Represented as a ram or as a man with the head of a ram.

_____ The jackal-looking god of mummification. It was he who led the dead into the underworld.

_____ English Egyptologist who helped discover the tomb of Tutankhamen.

_____ Builder of the great pyramid at Giza.

_____ Builder of the obelisk at Karnak and her temple at Deir el Bahari.

_____ Greek historian who traveled throughout Egypt.

_____ He was the sun-god of ancient Egypt; was shown as a falcon-headed god.

_____ He built the third pyramid at Giza.

_____ The first ruler of the Old Kingdom; united the two Egypts.

_____ Egyptian queen; wife of Amenhotep IV.

_____ A four-sided tapered monument with a pyramidal point; was usually made of red granite and dedicated to the sun-god.

_____ A cross with a loop at the top; the symbol of life.

_____ He was the god of the underworld.

_____ Egyptian sun-god; his chief symbol was the obelisk.

_____ Composite statue of the body of a lion and the head of a king.

_____ King of Egypt during the Eighteenth Dynasty; his tomb was discovered in 1922, yielding many treasures.

_____ He was responsible for building the "step" pyramid.

PART TWO/Egyptian, Mesopotamian, Aegean Art

Chronology: In the list below, cite the correct date for each entry.

Wheeled carts, Sumer _____

Upper and Lower Egypt united _____

Hieroglyphic writing, Egypt _____

Fall of Ur _____

Code of Hammurabi _____

Minoan civilization flourishes _____

Hebrews accept monotheism _____

Pyramid of Cheops _____

The Great Sphinx _____

Nefertiti _____

He-Goat from Ur _____

The Ishtar Gate _____

CHAPTER TWO

Mesopotamian Art

1. What characterized Mesopotamian cities for over three hundred years?

2. What are the predominant features of the monumental temple at Uruk (figs. 123, 124)? Compare it to the ziggurat at Ur (fig. 125).

3. Describe the secular relief bands on the alabaster vase from Uruk (fig. 126).

4. Characterize the sensitive facial features of the work entitled *Female Head* (fig. 127) by observing the thin-lipped mouth and oval eyes.

5. Describe the skirt, hair style, hands, and eyes in the cylindrical statues from the Abu temple (fig. 128).

6. What is the symbolic meaning of the bull located on the golden lyre in figure 129? Describe the scene on the end panel of this work.

7. What is the possible meaning of the rampant goat peering through the shrubbery in figure 130?

8. Describe the historical record (scene) in which Eannatum defeats his enemies in figure 131.

9. What are the portraitlike qualities contained in the *Head of an Akkadian Ruler* (fig. 132)?

10. Describe the dramatic scene in the *Stele of King Naram* (fig. 133) by stressing the form of the monument, the gazes of the soldiers, and their contorted postures.

11. Characterize the statuary during the Neo-Sumerian period as seen in figures 134 and 135 by using such terms as *chastised*, *pious*, *strength*, *calm*, and *wisdom*.

12. Detail the scene from the *Stele with the Code of Hammurabi* (fig. 137). Identify the sun god and the meaning of the rod and ring; describe Hammurabi's heavy dress.

13. Characterize the material and building techniques employed in the palace of Sargon II (fig. 140).

14. The giant winged bull-gods were integrated into the Gate at the Palace of King Sargon II (fig. 141). Describe their meaning and their timeless qualities.

15. Compare the *Portrait of King Sargon II* (fig. 142) with the calm, majestic *Head of Akkadian Ruler* (fig. 132).

16. The limestone relief from the palace of Nimrud (fig. 149) portrays what vivid scene? Such reliefs served what ornamental purpose?

17. In the *Dying Lions* (fig. 145) and *Herd of Fleeing Gazelles* (fig. 147), how has the artist shown his preoccupation with the problem of accurate observation?

18. Describe the brilliant glazed gate (fig. 147) of Nebuchadnezzar's palace.

19. How is the relief figure of *Darius and Xerxes Giving Audience* different from previous works done in the Near East?

20. Characterize the Persian rooms of Xerxes's great hall (fig. 151).

21. Describe the libation vessels in figures 152 and 153 by using terms such as *linear rhythm* and *grace*.

Study the *Time Line II* and complete the charts citing the significant art works of each society.

5000–2000 B.C.

	Painting	Sculpture	Architecture
Sumerian			
Egyptian (Archaic)			
Egyptian (Old Kingdom)			
Akkadian			

2000–1800 B.C.	Painting	Sculpture	Architecture
Neo-Sumerian			
Cycladic			
Egyptian (Middle Kingdom)			
Babylonian			

1800–1400 B.C.

	Painting	Sculpture	Architecture
Minoan			
Mycenaean			
Egyptian (New Kingdom)			

1400–600 B.C.

	Painting	Sculpture	Architecture
Hittite			
Assyrian			
Neo-Babylonian			
Persian			

CHAPTER THREE

Aegean Art

1. The term "Aegean" is conventionally used to describe the art of what civilizations?

2. Female marble figures (fig. 154) are regularly found in Cycladic graves, showing a stylized head with arms folded across the torso. How were these schematic, though recognizably human, forms different from previous examples of female figures?

3. Describe the intrinsic abstract appeal of the *Lyre Player* in figure 155.

4. Characterize the sophisticated Kamares style of pottery as exemplified in figure 156. Compare it to the more naturalistic figure in figure 157.

5. What was so revolutionary about Cretan palaces in both architectural and social terms as compared to earlier civilizations?

6. Explain the differences between the acrobatic bullfighters in figure 160 and the bull scenes in Egyptian and Mesopotamian art.

7. The use of natural themes is evident in what Minoan works of art?

8. Although technically primitive in anatomical naturalism, the two small *Boxers* (fig. 162) characterize a sense of pulsation. Explain.

9. Describe the Minoan iconography in the bare-breasted *Snake Goddess* (fig. 164). Symbolically, what does it represent?

10. Outline, movement, and naturalism are translated in the ivory *Acrobat* (fig. 165) as he leaps over a bull. Explain this statement.

11. Contrast and compare the figures on the small black vase known as the *Harvester* (fig. 166) to the regimented movement of Egyptian and Mesopotamian groups.

12. Describe the bull-head-shaped cup in figure 167.

13. In what ways were the palaces and tombs (figs. 168–171) on the mainland (Mycenaean) different from those of Minoan Crete?

14. Mycenaean craftsmen worked with gold, silver, and bronze to produce weapons (fig. 173), utility objects (figs. 174, 175), and luxury goods. Explain how these objects (fig. 172) may be considered works of art.

CHAPTER FOUR

Greek Art

1. Discuss what Pericles meant when he said, "Our love of what is beautiful does not lead to extravagance."

2. Discuss the terms *reason*, *objectivity*, *discipline*, *order*, and, most importantly, *restraint* in relation to *Classical art*.

3. Unlike the Egyptians, Greek artists were free from the restraint and domination of religious dogma. As a result, they began to see the beauties of this world and not the next world. Explain this statement.

4. How did Greek artists depict their gods in comparison to earlier civilizations?

5. How was Greek sculpture now free to portray the human body?

6. On what scale did architects begin to build monuments as man became more of an urbanite?

7. "Nothing in excess, and everything in proportion" may be one of the themes of Greek art. Explain.

8. List the periods of Greek art.

9. Describe the Mycenaean influence in early Greek temple building as seen in figure 178.

10. Discuss the terms *triangles*, *diamonds*, *swastikas*, and *bands* in relation to *Geometric* art.

11. Describe the funeral scene of the mourning women that appears on the amphora vase (fig. 179).

12. What is meant by the term *Proto-Attic style* as exemplified in figure 181?

13. An energetic style can be seen in the *Chigi Vase* (fig. 182). Explain this in relation to its size and depiction of the scene.

14. Describe the anatomical detail of the life-size sculpture known as *Lady of Auxerre.*

15. How important to western art were Greek islands containing marble?

16. Explain the style and terms *Kouros* and *Kore* that set the standard for Archaic sculpture.

17. In what way did Egyptian and Mesopotamian sculpture influence Archaic sculpture?

18. The *Calf-Bearer* (fig. 186) is considered the transitional work between the Kouros of Sounion and the Anavyssos Kouros. Explain.

19. How did the sculptor Aristokles free his figure (fig. 187) from Egyptian conventions?

20. Describe and compare the poses, drapery, and anatomical depictions of the female Korai in figures 188, 189, and 190.

21. Greek architecture, like sculpture, was intended to be seen by the public in open spaces, usually on an acropolis (mountain); therefore, the Greeks created an architecture that was never to be violent or gross in appearance. Explain this statement as it relates to Greek architecture.

22. What is the difference in purpose between Greek religious architecture and Egyptian religious architecture?

23. Greek civic architecture is sometimes referred to as the art of democratic Greece. What does this mean in relation to human scale?

24. Describe in detail the characteristics of the three orders of Greek architecture. Discuss the fourth order, known as the *composite*, which was favored by the Romans.

25. What part did sculpture play in Greek architecture as compared to Egyptian architecture?

26. What is so unusual about the temple of *Hera* (fig. 194)?

27. Describe the relief figure of Medusa (fig. 196) and compare it to the *Calf-Bearer* (fig. 186).

28. How has the sculptor shown a conception of the use of space in the *Battle of Gods and Giants* (fig. 197)?

29. How was the problem of creating two superimposed interior colonnades solved as shown in figure 200?

30. Describe the climax of Archaic sculpture by comparing the muscular movement and tension of the *Oriental Archer* (fig. 201), *Archer* (fig. 202), and the *Dying Warrior* (fig. 203).

31. How are Archaic vase paintings different from the ones from the Geometric period?

32. How has geometric ornamentation been reduced in the Dipylon Vase (fig. 179)?

33. Describe the scene in the work entitled *Dionysus in a Ship* (fig. 206).

34. What is the difference between "black-figure" technique and "red-figure" technique in vase painting?

35. Describe the scene from the *Iliad*, *Sarpedon Carried off the Battlefield*, in figure 207 by Eurphronios. Use the terms *line*, *richness*, and *refinement*.

36. Explain how *individuality* is one of the most important characteristics of Greek art during the Classical period.

37. What is the advantage of using bronze instead of marble for sculpture as exemplified in the *Charioteer* (fig. 210)?

38. What is so unique about the vertical position of the *Charioteer*?

39. Explain why the *Kritios Boy* (fig. 211) may be considered the transitional work from the Archaic to the Classical style of sculpture. Describe the significance of the bended knee and the shift of the body's weight to the other leg.

40. What is meant by the term *Severe style* and how was it applied to figure 212?

41. What makes the Zeus (fig. 213) an "idealized" statue?

42. Describe the tension and compression in the *Discus Thrower* (fig. 214).

43. How has the problem of the standing figure been solved in the *Spear Bearer* (fig. 215)?

44. Compare and contrast the naturalness of the *Two Warriors* in figures 217 and 218.

45. Feminine beauty is exalted in the *Birth of Aphrodite*. Use the term "wet drapery" to explain this statement.

46. What is the theme of the sculptured work entitled the *Battle of Lapiths and Centaurs*?

47. How was Polygnotos a great innovator in painting?

48. Describe the technique of fresco painting as exemplified in figure 227.

49. Artistically speaking, what is the significance of the Greek victory over the Persians?

50. Discuss why the Parthenon is sometimes referred to as the *sovereign* of the Acropolis. Use the terms *order*, *moderation*, *proportion*, and *unity* in your discussion.

51. Describe the east and west pediments of the Parthenon and what they represent.

52. What is the theme of the metopes depicting the mythological battle between the Greeks and the Amazons?

53. Describe the *Panathenaic Procession* in the frieze of the Parthenon.

54. The Athena Nike temple was erected between 427–424 B.C. and is considered the most elegant and graceful of the Ionic orders in classical antiquity. Explain and elaborate on this statement by including the relief entitled *Victory Untying Her Sandal* (fig. 243).

55. Describe the six Caryatids that support the entablature of the Erechtheion.

56. Describe the Phidian style in either *Victory* (fig. 247) or *Stele of Hegeso* (fig. 248).

57. What was so novel about the interior of the Temple of Apollo (fig. 249)?

58. What changes in classical art were ushered in as a result of the conquest of Alexander the Great? Use the circular building, outdoor theater, and mausoleum in your discussion.

59. Describe the first nude statue of Aphrodite (fig. 262).

60. How is the divine "ideal" in classical art represented in *Hermes Carrying the Child Dionysus* (fig. 263)?

61. What system of proportion did Lysippos introduce in his *Apoxyomenos* (fig. 264)?

62. In Greek painting, explain the techniques called *encaustic* and *tempera*.

63. What is a mosaic?

64. Describe the theme and scene of the mosaic called *Victory of Alexander over Darius III*.

65. How were cities planned differently during the Hellenic and Hellenistic periods of Greek history?

66. How was the problem of supporting a conical inner ceiling solved at Samothrace (fig. 272)?

67. Describe the Corinthian order in the Temple of Olympian Zeus (fig. 275).

68. Compare and contrast Hellenic and Hellenistic sculpture by examining the following works: *Portrait of Alexander*, *Demosthenes*, *Seated Boxer*, *Satyr*, and *Aphrodite of Cyrene*.

69. Describe the extraordinary torsion of the body in *Nike of Samothrace*. What does this work say about women during the Hellenistic period?

70. What is the symbolic meaning of the relief entitled *Battle of Gods and Giants* (fig. 284)?

71. Why is the Altar of Zeus (fig. 284) sometimes referred to as "Pergamene Baroque"? How is this style evident in the work entitled *Laocoon and His Two Sons* (fig. 287)?

72. Discuss the use of light and shadow in the *Infant Telephos* (fig. 290) and *Stag Hunt* (fig. 291).

73. Explain the technique known as *épousse* as it appears in the amphora (fig. 292).

PART TWO/CHAPTER FOUR

On the map indicate, by number, the approximate location of the following sites:

1. Segesta	**2.** Syracuse	**3.** Mt. Olympus
4. Delphi	**5.** Samothrace	**6.** Mycenae
7. Athens	**8.** Sparta	**9.** Rhodes
10. Chios	**11.** Knossos	**12.** Salonika

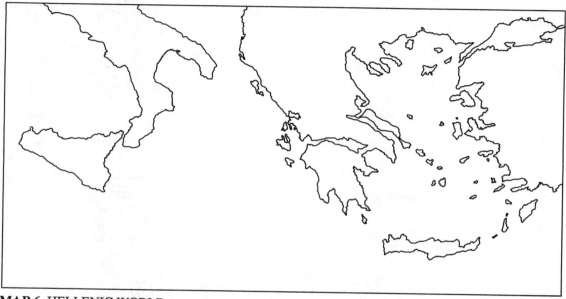

MAP 6. HELLENIC WORLD

Classical Architecture

Identify the four orders of Classical Architecture.

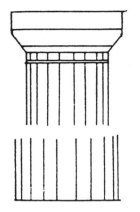

1. _____

2. _____

3. _____

4. _____

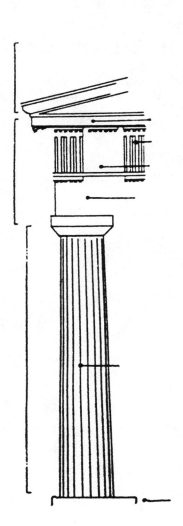

Label the following terms in their proper place:

Cornice

Triglyph

Metope

Architrave

Pediment

Frieze

Entablature

Column

Shaft

Base

Study the *Time Line III* and complete the chart by citing significant art works and historical events.

		Painting	Sculpture	Architecture	Historical Event
G E O M E T R I C	G R E E C E				
A R C H A I C	G R E E C E				
C L A S S I C A L	G R E E C E				
H E L L E N I S T I C	G R E E C E				

PART TWO/Greek Art

Chronology: Number the entries below in the correct chronological order beginning with number 3.

First tragedy performed at Athens by Thespis _____

Sparta defeats Athens _____

First Olympic Games ____2____

Trial and death of Socrates _____

Battle of Marathon _____

Alexander the Great founds Alexandria _____

Dorians invade Greece ____1____

Euclid _____

Death of Pericles _____

Archimedes _____

Eratosthenes of Cyrene measures the globe _____

Epic poems by Homer collected _____

Prepare a GLOSSARY from the list below by citing one name for each statement.

GLOSSARY

Exekias / Achilles / Erechtheion / Dionysus / Acropolis / Ajax / Kallikrates / Artemis / Amphora / Archaic art / Aphrodite / Hellenistic / Zeus / Hermes / Iktinos / Praxiteles / Nike / Olympia / Pericles / Phidias / Poseidon / Amazons

_____ In Greek legend, the hero of Homer's *Iliad*.

_____ In ancient Greece, it was the fortified citadel and elevated section of the city.

_____ In Greek legend, one of the heroes of the Trojan War who rescues the body of Achilles.

_____ In Greek mythology, a tribe of female warriors who fought against the Greeks. They were led by their leader Penthesilea.

_____ Vase used by the Greeks and Romans, consisting of a two-handled jar with a narrow neck to carry wine or water.

_____ In Greek religion, she was the goddess of love, beauty, and fertility.

_____ In Greek mythology, she was the twin sister of Apollo and the goddess of the moon and the hunt.

_____ He was the 5th-century Greek architect who helped build the Parthenon.

_____ God of wine.

_____ Temple on the Acropolis in Athens, built around 420 B.C.; it contains some of the finest examples of the Ionic order.

_____ A Greek painter and designer of amphora vases.

_____ A time in Greek history and culture from the rule of Alexander the Great (330 B.C.) to the first century B.C.

_____ In Greek mythology, the god of commerce, invention, and cunning who served as a messenger for other gods.

_____ Scene of the Olympic games and the center of worship of the god Zeus.

_____ Athenian statesman, orator, and general.

_____ Greek sculptor, considered by many the greatest artist in ancient Greece. His best works were done on the Parthenon.

_____ In Greek mythology, he was the god of water and earthquakes.

_____ In Greek mythology, he was ruler of the heavens and father of all other gods and mortal heroes.

Identify the following terms:

polis

_____
_____

symposia

_____
_____

amphora

_____
_____

archaic

_____
_____

kouros

_____
_____

kore

_____
_____

palestra

_____
_____

himation

_____
_____

peplos

_____
_____

peristyle

_____
_____

capital

_____
_____

abacus

_____
_____

echinus

_____
_____

volute

_____
_____

triglyphs

_____
_____

pediment

_____
_____

fasciae

_____
_____

drums

_____
_____

entasis

_____
_____

cella

_____
_____

prostyle

_____
_____

amphiprostyle

_____
_____

peristyle

_____

peripteral

_____

dipteral

_____

intercolumniation

_____

acroteria

_____

caryatids

_____

krater

_____

kylix

_____

parthenos

_____

propylaia

_____

Erechtheion

_____

orchestra

_____
_____

gynecaeum

_____
_____

encaustic

_____
_____

tempera

_____
_____

agora

_____
_____

bouleuterion

_____
_____

CHAPTER FIVE

Etruscan Art

1. Write a short essay outlining the Etruscans, the highest civilization in Italy before the rise of Rome.

2. Describe a typical Etruscan temple (fig. 294).

3. What engineering principle did the Etruscans borrow from the Greeks that became paramount in Roman architecture (fig. 295)?

4. Describe the typical funerary sculpture as in the Sarcophagus in figure 297.

5. Compare and contrast the *Apollo of Veii* with any Archaic Greek work.

6. What is the symbolic meaning of the bronze *She-Wolf* (fig. 299)? Compare it to the *Chimaera* (fig. 300).

7. Describe the engraved bronze mirror of Aphrodite (fig. 302). Discuss *line* in your description.

8. What is a cist? Briefly relate the story on the *Ficoroni Cist*.

9. Discuss the interior of a typical Etruscan tomb as exemplified in figures 304 and 305. Compare these to later tombs such as the burial chamber in figure 306.

On the map indicate, by number, the approximate location of the following sites:

1. Florence
2. Vetulonia
3. Cerveteri
4. Arezzo
5. Orvieto
6. Rome
7. Perugia
8. Vulci
9. Populonia
10. Veii

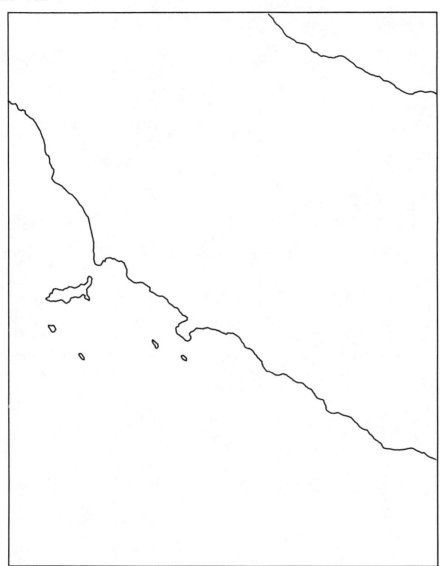

MAP 8. ETRURIA

CHAPTER 6

Roman Art

1. "Captive Greece took Rome captive." What does this statement mean when one looks at Roman art as a continuation of Greek classical traditions?

2. What was the purpose and meaning of Roman art? Use the terms *pragmatic*, *functional*, *grand in scale*, *political and ideological*, and *realistic* in your discussion.

3. What did the Romans borrow from the Etruscans in their building technique?

4. Unlike Greek public sculpture, early Roman sculpture took the form of a private portrait bust (death mask of a deceased person). Consequently, what individual characteristics were revealed in these masks that would become the hallmark of early Roman sculpture?

5. Concrete completely revolutionized architecture. What does it contain, and what advantages does it have once hardened and shaped?

6. Emperor Augustus claimed, "I found a city of brick and left it a city of marble." This statement may not be taken literally, but how did marble become an integral part of Roman architecture?

7. How are Roman places of worship different from the Egyptians' and the Greeks' places of worship? Include in your discussion design and execution, using the Temples of Fortuna Virilis and Sibyl as examples.

8. What new architectural thinking was introduced in the Sanctuary of Fortuna?

9. In what ways was the plan for the city of Pompeii similar to and different from a Greek agora plan?

10. Describe a basilica by using terms such as *nave*, *apse*, and *clerestory*.

11. Describe a private Roman house by using such terms as *atrium* and *tablinum*.

12. Describe the differences between the First and Second Pompeiian Styles of painting in which murals became an extension of architecture.

13. The aim of Roman sculpture was not to create the perfect, ideal, psychological Greek character study, but to depict the essence of the personality. Explain.

14. In the Villa of Mysteries (fig. 323), explain what is meant by *illusionary* painting.

15. In *Augustus of Prima Porta*, what part of the pose derives from the traditional Greek style? Describe the draped paludamentum around his hip and the embellished relief on his breastplate.

16. How does *official* monumental sculpture, as in the *Ara Pacis*, contain the historical, political, and ideological beliefs of the Roman Empire?

17. In what way is the *Ara Pacis* (fig. 329) typical of Pheidias's sculpture while it remains Roman at the same time?

18. In the *Imperial Procession* (fig. 329), one sees Augustus with his family, not as the conqueror, but as first citizen of Rome who is about to usher in a period of peace. Explain.

19. Describe the scene in the cameo the *Gemma Augustea* (fig. 331).

20. Describe the similarities of the Maison Carrée with the typical Greek style of architecture. What have the Romans added to this temple that was absent in Greek architecture?

21. Thomas Jefferson said of the Maison Carrée that he could gaze at it for hours, "like a lover at his mistress." Write a short essay on the Maison Carrée with this quotation in mind.

22. Discuss how Roman aqueducts are the finest examples of a synthesis between utilitarianism and aesthetics.

23. The finest example of hydraulic engineering and esthetic creativity is the *Pont du Gard* aqueduct (fig. 337). Explain this statement.

24. Explain why the Colosseum was the most sophisticated and largest elliptical amphitheater built in antiquity.

25. What makes the Colosseum aesthetically pleasing?

26. What was the purpose of the Arch of Titus, the final type of monumental architecture/sculpture?

27. Describe the triumphal procession (figs. 342, 343) in the interior of the Arch of Titus.

28. The Romans introduced into Western sculpture something that classical Greece could not do: the realistic depiction of men and women. Explain this statement after viewing figures 344, 345, and 374.

29. Explain why the illusionistic painting of the Third Style (figs. 346, 347) was the most complex type of architectural painting.

30. Describe Trajan's Column, the finest example of historical Roman relief sculpture. What does this pictorial document record?

31. What are the amazing engineering feats associated with the Pantheon? Discuss the problem of joining a circular building to a rectangular porch and triangular roof.

32. Compare and contrast the sculpture *Ceremonial Circular Gallop of the Cavalry* (fig. 362) with Trajan's Column.

33. What is the difference between Roman theaters and Greek theaters? Discuss *radial* and *enclosure*.

34. Describe the refined-looking portrait in figure 371.

35. Describe the size, scope, and function of the Baths of Caracalla. Discuss the lavish interior.

36. Discuss how the Basilica of Maxentius and Constantine (fig. 388) had an influence on the construction of the Basilica of Trier in Germany (figs. 391 and 392).

Study the *Time Line IV* and complete the chart by citing significant art works and historical events.

	Painting	Sculpture	Architecture	Historical Event
E T R U S C A N				
R O M A N / R E P U B L I C				
R O M A N / E M P I R E				
E A R L Y / C H R I S T I A N				

PART TWO/Roman Art

Identify the following Roman schematic plans:

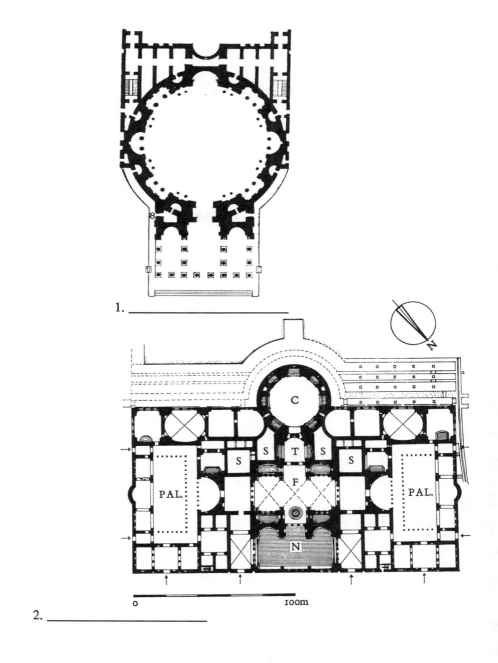

1. _____

2. _____

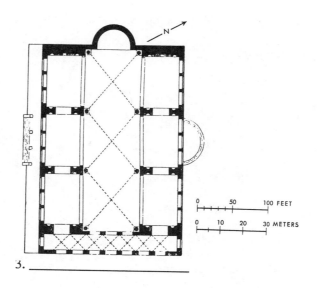

3. _____

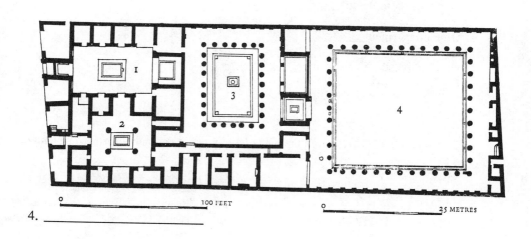

4. _____

Chronology: In the list below, cite the correct date for each entry.

First Punic War _____

Head of Pompey _____

First triumvirate _____

Augustus of Prima Porta _____

Caesar assassinated _____

Colosseum completed _____

Jesus Christ dies _____

Paul dies _____

Arch of Titus _____

Trajan rules _____

Ptolemy, astronomer, dies _____

Pantheon completed _____

Diocletian rules _____

Constantine the Great rules _____

Prepare a GLOSSARY from the list below by citing one name for each statement.

GLOSSARY

Titus / Severus / Agrippa / Augustus / Pliny / Marcella / Brutus / Magna Graecia / Portico / Podium / Hadrian / Cella / Caesar / Crassus / Caracalla / Trajan / Vespasian / Vitruvius

_____ Roman writer on architecture. His *De Architectura* was used by the architects of the Renaissance.

_____ Roman Emperor who waged war against the Jewish rebels. Began the building of the Colosseum.

_____ Roman Emperor from Spain who conquered much of Parthia.

_____ Son-in-law of Augustus who fought in the victorious war over Mark Antony at Actium.

_____ Great-nephew of Julius Caesar. He defeated Antony and Cleopatra at Actium, thus becoming master of the Roman world.

_____ The principal assassin of Julius Caesar who later committed suicide.

_____ Roman Emperor and military commander who was stabbed to death on March 15, 44 B.C.

_____ Roman Emperor who extended citizenship to all free inhabitants of the Empire. He was eventually murdered.

_____ Outside wall of a building.

_____ Member of the First Triumvirate (along with Caesar and Pompey) who was later murdered.

_____ Roman Emperor from Spain who built a wall in Britain.

_____ Roman consul and general who captured Syracuse in the Second Punic War.

_____ A great orator who became consul in 100 A.D.

_____ Steps of a building.

_____ The open entrance (roof) to the facade of a building.

_____ The Emperor of Rome from 306–307 A.D. who was killed by Maximillian at Ravenna.

_____ Roman Emperor who destroyed Jerusalem and completed the building of the Colosseum.

PART THREE

The Middle Ages

CHAPTER ONE

Early Christian And Byzantine Art

1. Describe and explain the function of the *domus* churches and martyriums of the Early Christian era.

2. What is the symbolic meaning of the ceiling fresco *The Good Shepherd* (fig. 397)?

3. Why is the wall painting of the interior of the Dura-Europas synagogue a remarkable work of art?

4. Discuss the significance of the Edict of Milan to Christianity and art.

5. Why did basilicas become the norm for church architecture after 313 A.D.?

6. How was old St. Peter's basilica different from the early Roman basilicas?

7. The *apse* of the church served what function in the Early Christian period?

8. State the purpose and describe the interior of the central plan for the basilica of Sta. Costanza, Rome.

9. How was Syrian architecture richer than its counterpart in the West during the Early Christian period?

10. Why were the wall surfaces of the Early Christian churches flat and free of sculpture or ornamentation?

11. Compare the use of mosaics of the Hellenistic and Roman periods with that of the Early Christian period. Give examples.

12. Why was the use of *tesserae* so important in Early Christian mosaics?

13. Describe the use of color mosaics in the Church of Hagios Georgios in Salonika, Greece.

14. Explain the meaning of the Annunciation mosaic at Sta. Maria Maggiore, Rome.

15. Why were illuminated manuscripts needed in the Early Christian church?

16. Describe the scenes in the sculptured *Sarcophagus of Junius Bassus*, as well as its theme.

17. How is the sense of the *dramatic* realized in the ivory panels entitled *The Three Marys at Sepulcher* and *The Ascension* (fig. 416)?

18. Describe briefly the history of the Roman Empire from 410 to 565 A.D. and its impact on art.

19. What important responsibility did Benedictine monks assume after 529 A.D.?

20. How has the appearance of Christ changed from the Early Christian period to the one entitled *Christ with Saints* in the Church of SS. Cosma e Damiano?

21. Explain why some art historians think that San Vitale is a beautiful microcosm of color and light.

22. Who are the retinue of dignitaries in the mosaic at San Vitale?

23. How did Byzantine architects solve the problem of placing a round dome over a square base?

24. Describe how the fusion of Christian, Oriental, Greek, and Roman motifs come together in Hagia Sophia.

25. What did Procopius mean when he said that the dome of Hagia Sophia was "let down from heaven on a golden chain"?

26. Describe one of the 104 carved capitals in Hagia Sophia.

27. Legend has it that when Emperor Justinian saw the interior of Hagia Sophia, he said, "Glory to God who has judged me worthy of accomplishing such a work as this! O Solomon, I have vanquished thee." Explain.

28. How do the real and spiritual worlds come together in the *Transfiguration* mosaic in the Monastery of St. Catherine, Egypt?

29. The word *icon* means *image*; any image of God, Christ, or the saints. Why did the Iconoclasts condemn the use of icons and how was the issue finally resolved?

30. In the icon of *Virgin and Child* at St. Catherine on Mount Sinai, why are the figures rigid, unrealistic, and non-three-dimensional?

31. What is the meaning of the term *Pantocrator* as seen in the icon in the Church of St. Catherine? Describe it.

32. Why was ivory chosen as an ideal medium for secular as well as religious objects of art?

33. Mary and Jesus are set in an earthly architectural ivory diptych (fig. 346). How do they seem to disassociate themselves from the material earthly world?

34. What was the Macedonian Renaissance?

35. Explain the uniqueness of the *Joshua Roll* and *Paris Psalter* illustrated manuscripts.

36. Compare the size, interior, and exterior of the *Hosios Loukas* monastery with those of the early Christian era.

37. Characterize the 12th-century mosaics entitled the *Crucifixion* and *Pantocrator* in the Church of Dormiton, Daphni.

38. List the Gothic, Romanesque, and Byzantine characteristics in the Cathedral of Venice.

39. How is Christ portrayed as a Roman emperor in the Cathedral of Cefalu?

40. Describe the style of paintings in the church of Saint Pantalemon at Nerezi.

41. Explain the technique called *secco su fresco* and give examples.

42. What is the theme of the *Anastasis* apse fresco (fig. 455)?

43. Choose any Russian church or painting in the Byzantine style and describe its Russian characteristics.

CHAPTER TWO

Islamic Art

1. The meaning and purpose of Islamic art is summarized in one word, *Islam*. Define this word and its impact on Islamic art and society.

2. Islamic architecture, like its art, may also be summarized in one word, *mosque*. Define this word and all the important architectural elements contained in it.

3. What is the significance of the shrine called *The Dome of the Rock* for Moslems and for art?

4. In the *Palace of Shapur* (fig. 463), what very important structure was introduced that had a tremendous impact on Western architecture? Describe it.

5. Since the Koran prohibited images of living figures, except in private places, how did Islamic artists decorate interior walls? Give examples.

6. State the purpose of minarets and describe the Mesopotamian influences in the spiral minaret at Samarra (fig. 467).

7. The Great Mosque at Cordoba was built by Abd ar-Rahman, who said, "My mosque shall be a forest of psalms." Explain this statement as it relates to his mosque.

8. What are *madrasahs* in Islamic civilization? Describe one from an architectural point of view.

9. Describe the beauty and state the significance of the inner court of the Alhambra, known as the *Court of the Lions*.

10. What part did stylized calligraphy letters from verses of the Koran play in Islamic art?

11. State the meaning and purpose of the *Taj Mahal*. Describe this unique structure as a symbol of Indian Islamic art.

12. Explain the meaning of the illuminated Islamic manuscripts entitled the *Temptation of Adam and Eve* and *Bihzad in the Garden*. Compare these with Christian interpretations.

CHAPTER THREE

Barbarian And Christian Art
In Northern Europe

1. What is the misnomer about the *Dark Ages* in Western civilization?

2. The term *Barbarian art* means "foreign." Describe the main characteristics of this art form by using such terms as *abstract*, *geometrical*, and *zoomorphic*.

3. From Celtic art, show how women played a very important role in the civilization.

4. How did Persian art influence Barbarian art? Give one example.

5. Characterize the metalwork in figure 486 and compare it to the stone shaft-figure from Holzgerlinger, Germany (fig. 487).

6. Explain the beauty and significance of the *Gundestrup Caldron* silver bowl (fig. 488).

7. Briefly state the technique used in the metal objects known as the *Panther* (fig. 489) and *Scythian plaque* (fig. 490).

8. Describe the zoomorphic interlacing of the Purse Lid from the Sutton Hoo ship.

9. Why is the Stern Post of the Osberg ship so pleasing and complex a work of art? What feeling was it meant to create in the eyes of the viewer?

10. In what way did *Illuminated Manuscripts* artistically contain the word of God?

11. Describe what artists and calligraphy writers would do with the first letter of a handwritten book to make an illuminated manuscript.

12. In the *Lindisfarne Gospels*, explain how intricate patterns are made up from lacertine and interlaced motifs.

13. Why is the *Book of Kells* one of the most beautifully decorated books in Western civilization? Describe the dynamic decorations.

14. What conclusions can one draw about Barbarian art and society from the small quantity it produced?

CHAPTER FOUR

The Art Of The Holy Roman Empire

1. Why is Charlemagne referred to as "Charles the Great"?

2. In the Palatine Chapel of Aachen, what are the similarities and differences between it and its counterpart, San Vitale?

3. What was the Carolingian Renaissance?

4. How did the architect create a sense of dignity in the little Abbey of Lorsch?

5. Explain and give examples of the instructions that Charlemagne laid down for mural painting and mosaics.

6. Describe the Classical manner in which the Evangelist Matthew is portrayed in figure 502 and compare it to the *Saint Matthew* in the *Ebbo Gospels* (fig. 504).

7. Why is the *Utrecht Psalter* considered a masterpiece of Western art?

8. Describe the function of color in the *Bible of Charles the Bald*.

9. What were the covers for illuminated Christian codex made of? Give examples.

10. Explain how the five Ottonian rulers (919–1024) brought artistic leadership to Germany. Give examples.

11. What are the two new style traits found in Ottonian architecture?

12. State the theme of the massive bronze doors of the Cathedral of Hildesheim.

13. Describe how the Column of Bishop Bernward (fig. 515) is similar to Imperial Roman columns in narration.

14. What is so unique about the sculptured Crucifix of Archbishop Gero? Describe it.

15. Explain what is meant by spatial relationship as exemplified in the *Otto Imperator Augustus* manuscript (fig. 518).

16. Show how the real and unreal come together in the *Annunciation to Shepherds*.

17. The imagination of the artist comes out in the illuminated *Vision of Isaiah.* Explain.

18. Characterize the *Hitda Codex* and *Uta Codex.*

CHAPTER FIVE

Romanesque Art

1. What is the meaning of the word *Romanesque* and how was this term applied to architecture?

2. What is the symbolic meaning of the word *nave*?

3. Explain the following terms: *barrel vault*, *groined vault*, and *rib vault*.

4. What Roman technique of vaulting was not used by Romanesque architects?

5. Describe the balance that Romanesque architects were trying to achieve in their buildings.

6. How was the problem of *stress* support solved in the Abbey Church of St.-Philibert (fig. 523)?

7. What was the purpose of ambulatories in pilgrimage churches?

8. Explain the effect a continuous barrel vault has on a viewer.

9. What is the function of the compound pier?

10. Give the statistical dimensions of the staggering Church of Saint-Pierre at Cluny.

11. What is a triforium arch? Give an example.

12. Describe the drapery, pose, and meaning of the sculptured capital in figure 529.

13. Explain what vaulting solution was used at Vézelay to span its entire nave.

14. Briefly describe the scene in the tympanum at Ste.-Madeleine (fig. 531).

15. Why is the abstract-designed sculpture of the *Last Judgment* (fig. 532) so awesome a scene?

16. In the tympanum of St. Pierre in Mossac, describe the appearance of Christ, the symbols of the evangelists, and the twenty-four Elders. What is the significance of this work for future sculpture during the Romanesque period?

17. Explain how a tragic sense of emotion was made visible in the *Descent from the Cross* (fig. 536).

18. Pick out the classical and unclassical characteristics in the triple portal of the Priory Church in figure 537.

19. What happened to the entire facade of the Church of Notre-Dame-la-Grande at Poitiers?

20. Why is the *Renier De Huy* baptismal font (fig. 539) considered the most classical example of Romanesque sculpture of this period?

21. What color combination was used for the facade of many Italian Romanesque structures?

22. Discuss the shape, color, and exterior of the Baptistery of Florence, the facade of S. Minialto al Monte, and the Baptistery and Cathedral of Pisa in relation to classical art.

23. Explain why Sicilian art is a juxtaposition of many styles. Use the Cathedral of Monreale as an example.

24. Describe what makes the sculptured scenes (fig. 546) by Wiligelmo Da Modena so unique. Compare them with the work done by Benedetto Antelami (figs. 547, 548).

25. What new method of vaulting was introduced in the Cathedral of Speyer that was different from the classical Roman technique?

26. Explain the statement that "the groin vault has now been provided with ribs *along the groins*" (fig. 554).

27. Discuss and describe why the interior of Durham Cathedral is "one of the most forceful . . . of the Middle Ages."

28. In what way did the Abbey Church of Saint-Etienne set the stage for Gothic architecture and what structural innovation was introduced here?

29. Describe the dramatic and decorative Italian Romanesque wall paintings entitled the *Crucifixion* (fig. 560) and *Christ Enthroned* (fig. 561).

30. Compare the above cycle of paintings with the wall paintings done in France at Berze-la-Ville (fig. 564) and in Spain at Tahull (fig. 563).

31. Characterize two of the following regional styles of Romanesque illuminated manuscripts: The Gospels of Saint-Bertin, the Beatus Manuscripts, Citeaux, the Bible of Bury St. Edmunds and Saint Hildegarde of Bingen (pages 436–441).

32. State the historical and technical background of the *Bayeux Tapestry*.

CHAPTER SIX

Gothic Art

1. Renaissance architects considered any art that did not follow the canons of classical art as barbaric (Gothic). Explain this statement.

2. How are lightness, grace, and femininity of style characteristics of Gothic art?

3. Explain the term *opus francigenum* and how it took on an "international style."

4. Gothic art made its first breakthrough in architecture when Abbot Suger built the Church of St. Denis. What structural technique was introduced here that became the norm throughout the Gothic period?

5. Explain what Abbot Suger meant when he said that "Man can understand absolute beauty, which is God, only through the effect of precious and beautiful things on the senses."

6. Explain how Chartres Cathedral stands midway between the Late Romanesque and the High Gothic.

7. Interpret the following words of Henry Adams, who wrote that Chartres "expressed an emotion, the deepest man every felt . . . , the struggle of man's own littleness to grasp the infinite."

8. Describe how the cylindrical statues (fig. 596) blend so easily with the structure behind them.

9. Explain the mystical significance of the number seven.

10. Describe the dramatic facade of Laon Cathedral.

11. What was the purpose of choir screens in churches?

12. Compare and contrast the facade of Laon Cathedral with that of Notre-Dame in Paris. Explain why the facade of Notre-Dame creates a sense of complete equilibrium.

13. Chartres is unique because it was the first church to have been planned from start to finish with the idea of using flying buttresses. Explain this statement.

14. In the sculptured figure 587, immobile and columnar statues appear to be alive and sensitive. Explain.

15. Abbot Suger had high praise for the use of light when he said, "For dear is what is joined clearly with clear, and clear is the noble work that is irradiated with new light." What does this statement mean in relation to stained glass windows of Gothic cathedrals?

16. Figure 588 is called the *Belle Verrière*, the "Beautiful One" of the stained glass windows. State to whom this window is dedicated, what its shape is, and describe the glowing use of colors that dominates the scene.

17. Compare and contrast the naves and aisles of the Cathedral of Bourges with those of Notre-Dame of Paris.

18. What makes the exterior of Le Mans one of the most daring structures of medieval architecture?

19. What is the historical significance of Reims Cathedral?

20. Reims is a realm of stone, consisting of over five thousand statues. Explain this statement.

21. Describe the consistent unity and beauty of Reims's nave.

22. In the *Annunciation and Visitation* jamb statues (fig. 594), explain the style and meaning. Compare them to *The Knight's Communion* (fig. 595).

23. Describe the interior of the Cathedral of Amiens in terms of proportion, delicacy, and *rayonnant* style.

24. In what way is the sculptured statue of *Christ Treading on the Lion and the Basilisk* different from the traditional version of him as the awesome Pantocrator? Use the term "le beau Dieu" in your discussion.

25. The interior of Sainte-Chapelle in Paris is a tour de force in art. Explain why this is so.

26. Describe how God is portrayed as the perfect architect in the *Bible Moralisée* (fig. 12).

27. Describe the excitement, elegance, and tracery in the manuscript entitled *Psalter of Saint Louis* (fig. 607).

28. What is meant by the term "Flamboyant style of architecture"? Cite an example by describing the domestic mansion of Jacques Coeur (fig. 608).

29. Explain how the lassitude and courtly aloofness of sculpture are expressed in the *Virgin of Paris* (fig. 608).

30. In what way is the Belleville Breviary different from an ordinary one containing the readings for the Divine Offices?

31. Describe both the similarities and differences between the Cologne Cathedral and French cathedrals. Cite examples from both the exteriors and the interiors.

32. Why were flying buttresses unnecessary in the Church of St. Elizabeth at Marburg?

33. How has the issue of whether Nicholas of Verdun is a Romanesque or Early Gothic sculptor been settled? In what way is his work reminiscent of Hellenistic sculpture?

34. The individuality of German Gothic sculpture is evident in *Death of the Virgin* (fig. 616), *Angels* (fig. 617), *Ekkehard and Uta* (fig. 618), and *Rider* (fig. 619). Explain this statement by choosing one of the sculptured pieces mentioned and describing its individuality.

35. What is the symbolic meaning of the work entitled *Woman of the Apocalypse*?

36. In the Cathedral of Gerona, Spain (fig. 621), how have the Spanish reinterpreted French Gothic to serve their own needs?

37. In what ways are English Gothic cathedrals different from their French counterparts? Use the plan, nave, and exterior of Salisbury Cathedral as examples.

38. Explain why Gloucester Cathedral has one of the most complex vaulting systems in Gothic architecture, using the term *perpendicular* in your discussion.

39. In the Chapel of Henry VII (fig. 626), describe the multiplicity of extra ribs in the form of a fan.

40. Briefly describe the depiction and meaning in the Wilton diptych.

41. Why does the interior of the Gothic Abbey of Fossanova in Italy seem so austere compared to French Gothic interiors?

42. What differentiates Italian Gothic cathedrals from the complex and soaring forest of pointed arches in French Gothic cathedrals? In your discussion, include the use of geometric plans, buttresses, semicircular arches, vaults, wall painting, and facades.

43. Describe the *rayonnant* style of architecture in the windows of Milan's cathedral.

44. Compare the psychological and defensive effect the facade of the Palazzo Vecchio in Florence (fig. 637) has on the viewer with the effect of the elegant Palazzo Ducale in Venice (fig. 638). Bring the words *mass* and *color* into your discussion.

45. The use of light, color, and interlaced arches makes the Ca' d'Oro in Venice thoroughly Italian Gothic. Explain this statement.

On the map indicate, by number, the approximate location of the following sites:

1. Madrid	2. Paris	3. St. Gilles
4. Venice	5. Rouen	6. Pisa
7. Moissac	8. Amiens	9. Rome
10. Cluny	11. Reims	12. Palermo
13. Bourges	14. Speyer	15. Salisbury
16. Chartres	17. Vienna	18. Canterbury

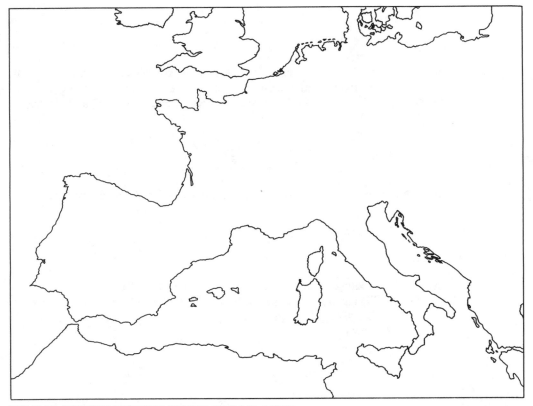

MAP 11. EUROPE IN THE HIGH MIDDLE AGES

Define the following terms and, if possible, cite a work of art in which they appear.

dogma

_____

_____

monasticism

_____

_____

feudal system

_____

_____

cathedra

_____

_____

scholasticism

_____

_____

missa

_____

_____

episkopoi

_____

_____

domus ecclesia

_____

_____

martyrium

_____

_____

columbaria

_____

_____

tesserae

_____

_____

codex

_____

_____

rotuli

_____

_____

squinches

_____

_____

buttresses

icon

Pantocrator

diptychs

Iconoclasts

Iconodules

Christus patiens

Deësis

secco su fresco

Islam

sahn

qibla

mihrab

minbar

arabesque

colonnettes

_____

barbarian

_____

_____

imago hominis

_____

_____

campanile

_____

Gothic

_____

_____

Romanesque

_____

_____

breviary

_____

loggia

_____

_____

nave

_____

apse

_____

_____

clerestory

_____

domus

_____

_____

atrium

_____

tablinum

_____

_____

imperator

_____

_____

pontifex maximus

_____
_____

insula

_____
_____

nymphaea

_____
_____

PART THREE/Medieval Art

Identify the following Gothic schematic plans.

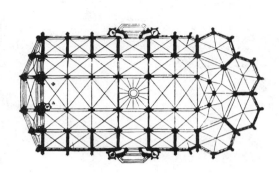

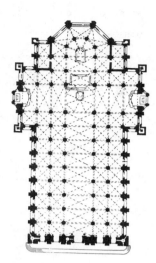

1. _____

2. _____

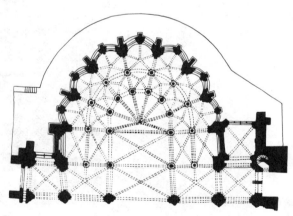

3. _____

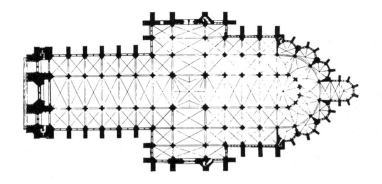

4. _____

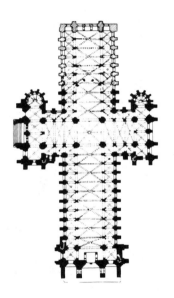

5. _____

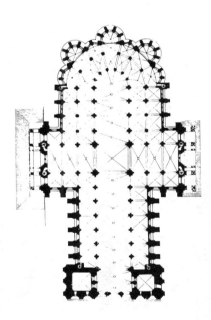

6. _____

Complete the chart by describing the different Gothic architectural styles.

	Example of Work	Characteristics
French Gothic		
English Gothic		
Italian Gothic		

Quotations: From the following list, cite the work of art associated with the quotations below.

Noli me tangere (fig. 589) / *Annunciation* (fig. 416) / *Christ Enthroned* (fig. 561) / *Doubting Thomas* (fig. 517) / *The Good Shepherd* (fig. 397) / *Christ icon* (fig. 433) / *Lorsch Gospels* (fig. 508) / *Annunciation* (fig. 443) / Apse, Cathedral of Cefalu (fig. 450) / *Pantocrator* (fig. 445)

_____ "I am the good shepherd; the good shepherd giveth his life for the sheep."

_____ "The Holy Ghost shall come upon thee, and the power of the Highest shall overshadow thee."

_____ "light of men"

_____ "a man of sorrows and acquainted with grief."

_____ "And when she saw him, she was troubled at his saying, and cast in her mind what manner of salutation this should be."

_____ "Surely he hath borne our griefs, and carried our sorrows."

_____ "I am the light of the world. . . ."

_____ "Thou shalt tread upon the lion and the adder: the young lion and the dragon shalt thou trample under foot."

_____ "Reach hither thy finger. . . ."

_____ "And there was war in heaven: Michael and his angels fought against the dragon. . . ."

_____ "Do not touch me. . . ."

PART THREE/Gothic Art

Chronology: Number the entries below in the correct chronological order beginning with number 2.

Fourth Crusade _____

Canterbury Tales by Chaucer _____

St. Francis founds Franciscan order _____

Boccaccio writes *Decameron* _____

Greeks retake Constantinople from Latins _____

Papacy moves to Avignon _____

University of Oxford _____1_____

Magna Carta signed in England _____

Earliest known use of cannon _____

St. Thomas Aquinas' *Summa Theologica* _____

Albertus Magnus _____

PART THREE/Medieval Art

Prepare a GLOSSARY from the list below by citing one name for each statement.

GLOSSARY

Trivium / Bouteroue / Transept / Suger / Clerestory / Jamb / Flamboyant / Straining Arch / Portals / Flying Buttress / Gislebertus / Groin Vault / Rayonnant / Quadrivium / Nave / Voussoirs / Tympanum / Trumeau / Ambulatory / Zoomorphic / Star Vaulting / Arabesque / Pendentive / Pantocrator / Diptych / Elousa / Icon / Mihrab / Manara / Iconoclast / Justinian / Maksoura / Madrasah / Stalactile

_____ French for buttress. It was the projecting structure of masonry for supporting a wall.

_____ An outside wall of a church that rises above an adjoining roof containing windows.

_____ Characterized by waving curves to suggest flames.

_____ An arch or half-arch projecting from the wall of a building to give additional strength.

_____ Sculptor of *The Last Judgment* at Autun, France.

_____ The intersection of two equal vaults coming together at right angles.

_____ An upright column forming the side of a door.

_____ Latin for ship; the center aisle of a church.

_____ Use of radiating lines in 14th-century French architecture, particularly in window tracery.

_____ The upper division of the seven liberal arts during the Middle Ages, consisting of arithmetic, music, geometry, and astronomy.

_____ Ornate doorways.

_____ An inverted double arch.

_____ Abbot and builder of Saint-Denis, which is considered by many to be the first Gothic church.

_____ The center crossing of a church.

_____ A group of studies forming the lower division of the seven liberal arts, consisting of grammar, rhetoric, and logic.

_____ The center pillar of a portal that divides a doorway.

_____ The space within an arch and above a lintel.

_____ Wedge-shaped stones used to construct an arch.

_____ A sheltered walkway found in churches, cloisters, and mosques.

_____ A style in Islamic art that employs flowers, foliage, and animals to produce an intricate design.

_____ In Byzantine art, a two-leaf, hinged tablet folded together to protect the writing in its interior.

_____ The portrayal of the Madonna in Byzantine art with affection and compassion.

_____ A religious image painted on wooden panels used in the devotion by Eastern Christians.

_____ It was one who destroyed religious images or opposed their veneration during the early part of Byzantine history.

_____ Byzantine Emperor who built the Church of Hagia Sophia and who is also remembered for his codification of Roman law.

_____ Open courtyard bordered by four arcades.

_____ An enclosed prayer hall in Islamic art.

_____ In Byzantine art, the depiction of Christ holding an open book or blessing with his right hand.

_____ The concave space formed when a horizontal quarter-circle supports a dome over a square space.

_____ Islamic vaulting consisting of layers of brick scalloped out to resemble natural stalactites.

_____ Islamic innovation of creating a dome within a dome.

_____ An art style having the form of an animal.

PART FOUR

The Renaissance

CHAPTER ONE

The Dawn Of Individualism in Italian Art—The Thirteenth And Fourteenth Centuries

1. What books on art were written by Ghiberti, Vasari, and Cennini?

2. Explain the term *burgher artisans.*

3. Explain the significance of Pisa in the latter Middle Ages.

4. How did Nicola Pisano show the Renaissance characteristic of *individuality* in his marble pulpit in the Baptistery at Pisa (figs. 640, 641)?

5. In what way did Giovanni Pisano combine elements of Italian Medieval art with Northern Gothic style (figs. 642–644)?

6. How different is Giovanni's pulpit at Pistoia from his father's at Pisa?

7. How did Giovanni show himself a master of free narrative?

8. Explain the importance of new religious ritual changes in the 13th century and their impact on art.

9. Describe how Cimabue tried to put the effects of Byzantine mosaics in his *Madonna Enthroned* (fig. 645).

10. What effect did the papacy have on Roman art when it moved from Rome to Avignon in France?

11. Describe the effect of light on Cavallini's *Last Judgment* (fig. 646).

12. In what way did Cavallini influence the works of Giotto?

13. Interpret the following quotation from Dante's *Purgatory*: "Cimabue believed that he held the field in painting, and now Giotto has the cry, so that the fame of the former is obscure."

14. Why did Vasari call Giotto "the pupil of Nature"?

15. Discuss the significance of weight and mass in Giotto's *Madonna and Child Enthroned* (fig. 647).

16. Explain what is meant by the phrase that Giotto translated ". . . painting from Greek to Latin."

17. Describe how Giotto conquered solid forms on a flat surface.

18. Outline how a fresco is built section by section.

19. Summarize the pictorial drama in Giotto's *Raising of Lazarus* and the *Lamentation* (figs. 648, 649).

20. How is a sense of calmness achieved in the *Lamentation* through the use of a diagonal line?

21. What is the symbol of the Trinity in Gaddi's *Annunciation to the Shepherds* (fig. 650)? What is its significance at the end of the Middle Ages?

22. Indicate the Byzantine traditions found in Duccio's *Virgin as Queen of Heaven* (fig. 651) and the effects of Pisano on Duccio's works.

23. What is the Sienese contribution to the history of art in the field of landscape? Give examples.

24. Identify the new techniques used by the Lorenzettis to create the illusion of depth in their painting *Birth of the Virgin* (fig. 653).

25. Describe the flamboyant style in Martini's *Annunciation* (fig. 657).

26. How are the results of the Black Death reflected in the work of Traini?

27. What is the intent of the word *pietà*? How effectively was this used in Giovanni da Milano's painting (fig. 660)?

PART FOUR/Italian Renaissance

On the map indicate, by number, the approximate location of the following works of art:

1. Ospedale degli Innocenti
3. *Allegory of Good Government*
5. Monument of Gattamelata
7. Pisano's *Adoration of the Magi*
9. Palazzo degli Uffizi
11. *Arrival of Cardinal Francesco Gonzaga*
13. Sta. Maria delle Carceri

2. Malatesta Temple
4. Tempieto, S. Pietro
6. Villa Rotonda
8. Library of S. Marco
10. *Dead Christ*
12. Sant'Andrea
14. Bellini's *Transfiguration of Christ*

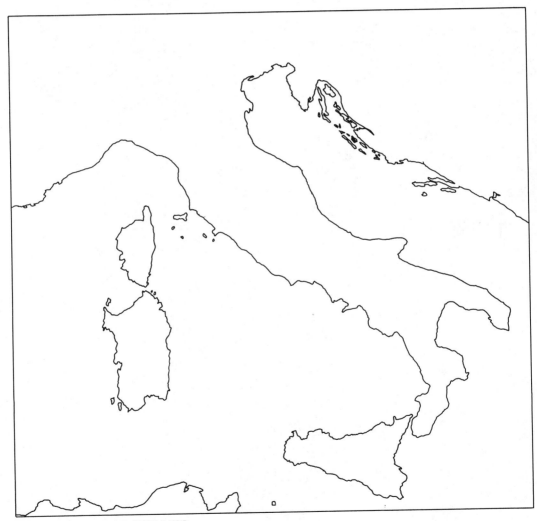

Map 12. ITALY ABOUT 1500

CHAPTER TWO

The Early Renaissance In Italy—
The Fifteenth Century

1. Define the term *Renaissance* as it relates to classical literature.

2. Who was Francesco Petrarca?

3. In what field of art did 15th-century Italian artists adopt a classical Roman vocabulary? Explain your answer.

4. What did Jakob Burckhart mean by "The Discovery of the World and of Man" in his work *The Civilization of the Renaissance in Italy*?

5. What is the theme of Manetti's work, *On the Dignity and Excellence of Man*?

6. State the three new phenomena of Renaissance art that were seldom seen in Medieval art.

7. Explain the position of women in Renaissance art and politics.

8. What Renaissance men were diversified artists?

9. Why was the Gothic tradition still strong in Northern Europe until the High Renaissance?

10. Describe the Gothic characteristics of Brunelleschi's Duomo for the Cathedral of Florence (fig. 661).

11. Describe the classical elements of Brunelleschi's lantern for the Duomo.

12. How is a sense of proportion created in Brunelleschi's Ospedale degli Innocenti (fig. 662)?

13. Where is the vanishing point in Brunelleschi's interior for the Church of San Lorenzo in Florence (fig. 664)?

14. Why is Brunelleschi's Pazzi Chapel referred to as the "architecture of humanism" (figs. 666–668)?

15. What are the Classical elements in Michelozzo's Palazzo Medici-Riccardi in Florence (fig. 669)?

16. Compare Alberti's facade of the Palazzo Ruccellai (fig. 672) and Michelozzo's Palazzo.

17. In the Malatesta Temple by Alberti (fig. 673), why is the facade so effective in creating a sense of grandeur?

18. What classical characteristics of Alberti's interior of Sant'Andrea (fig. 674) had an influence on future architects such as Bramante?

19. Describe the similarities between the Pazzi Chapel and Sangallo's Church of Santa Maria delle Carceri at Prato (figs. 677, 678).

20. In what way did political freedom and self-dignity play a part in Renaissance sculpture?

21. In what work by Donatello is his style clearly defined? Describe it.

22. How was a sense of tension created in Donatello's *St. George* (fig. 680)?

23. What technique did Donatello use in his work *Saint George and the Dragon* (fig. 681) that marked the separation in art between the ideal and the optical?

24. According to Vasari, Donatello was supposed to have said to his statue *Habakkuk*, "Speak, damn you, speak. Why will you not speak?" How does this statue speak for itself (fig. 682)?

25. The equestrian statue of the mounted *condottiere* by Donatello was based on the antique statue of Marcus Aurelius. Yet what makes this work thoroughly Renaissance in its characteristics (fig. 685)?

26. Describe how Donatello makes ugliness an artistic expression in the form of art in his *St. Mary Magdalene* (fig. 686).

27. In what way are the *Gates of Paradise* (figs. 689, 690), name coined by Michelangelo, a masterpiece of the "painter in bronze," Lorenzo Ghiberti?

28. Explain the political theme of Nanni di Banco's *Four Crowned Martyrs* (fig. 691).

29. What technique did Luca Della Robbia invent for producing architectural sculpture (fig. 692)?

30. Describe the heroic action taking place in Jacopo Della Quercia's *Expulsion from Eden* (fig. 694).

31. Give examples of the revolutionary ideas introduced in Gentile da Fabriano's *Adoration of the Magi* (fig. 695).

32. Like Giotto, how did Masaccio break with the Gothic style of painting thin and fragile figures (figs. 687–701)?

33. In the tradition of the Florentine school of art, what technique did Fra Angelico use to create strong, pious scenes in his paintings (figs. 702, 703)?

34. What makes Fra Filippo Lippi's paintings look so worldly in appearance (figs. 704, 705)?

35. Paolo Uccello is reported to have said to his wife, ". . . how charming a thing is this perspective; ah, if I could only get you to understand its delights." With this quotation in mind, how was perspective used to create the third dimension in the *Rout of San Romano* (fig. 707)?

36. How is one-point perspective used to its full advantage in the *Saint Lucy Altarpiece* by Veneziano (fig. 708)?

37. In Castagno's *Last Supper* (fig. 710), there was no one-point perspective, yet a sense of depth was created. Explain how this was achieved.

38. How was a sense of balance, calmness, and quiet dignity created in Piero Della Francesca's *Resurrection* (fig. 712) and his *Meeting of Solomon and the Queen of Sheba* (fig. 713)?

39. Describe how Classical and Christian elements came together in the *Tomb of Leonardo Bruni* by Rossellino (fig. 716).

40. In what way is the portrait bust of Giovanni Chellini (fig. 718) by Antonio Rossellino different from previous ones?

41. Who was the finest sculptor of children during the Renaissance in Italy? Describe the soft, atmospheric effect he created.

42. Who was Savonarola and what impact did he have on Florentine art and politics?

43. In the *Martyrdom of Saint Sebastian* (fig. 720) by Pollaiuolo, show how the composition was built up from *action* rather than *arrangement* of the figures.

44. Explain how the dynamic was achieved in *Hercules and Antaeus* (fig. 722).

45. What effect did Verrocchio depend on in his *Doubting of Thomas* (fig. 723) and the *Colleoni* (fig. 724)? Compare his works with those of Donatello.

46. The inspiration for the *Birth of Venus* (fig. 726) was provided by Poliziano, the humanist poet and friend of Botticelli, from his poem *The Joust*. Venus, for Poliziano and other neoplatonic poets, represented *humanitas*. What humanistic virtues does she possess in this painting?

47. Would you agree or disagree that *Venus* is an enticing nude by Botticelli? What makes the pose Classical, yet very Gothic in appearance?

48. Explain the allegorical meaning of the painting *Primavera* (fig. 725) based on the following quotation by Poliziano: "*Per domani non c'e' centezza*" ("For tomorrow it is uncertain").

49. What makes the *Primavera* and Botticelli "the most fateful of all exponents of feminine beauty," according to Kenneth Clark?

50. Describe how Ghirlandaio depicts the feeling of *bourgeois* in his *Birth of the Virgin* (fig. 727).

51. Compare the figures in Perugino's *Giving of the Keys to Saint Peter* (fig. 728) with Ghirlandaio's work.

52. How are anatomy and perspective joined to become the subject of Mantegna's *Dead Christ* (fig. 733)?

53. How has a traditional religious subject become a portrait of Classical and contemporary Italy in *Saint James Led to Execution* (fig. 730)?

54. Describe the Northern European characteristics found in the work of the Sicilian painter Antonello da Messina (fig. 734).

55. What technique did Bellini use to create a softening effect in his painting *Transfiguration of Christ* (fig. 736)?

CHAPTER THREE

The Early Renaissance
In Northern Europe

1. Explain what Italians thought about Northern European architecture and painting.

2. What part did Philip the Bold play in the development of Northern European painting.

3. Discuss the ways in which French and Italian relations were very strong.

4. Describe how the painter Sluter imbued his figures with expressive strength (figs. 737–739).

5. Compare the *Annunciation and Visitation* (fig. 740) of Broederlam with the style of Sluter's sculptured figures and the Boucicaut Master's *Visitation*.

6. Explain how the Limbourgs abandoned the traditional Byzantine background for a real three-dimensional one in their illuminated manuscripts (fig. 743).

7. Show how architectural and agricultural landscapes are blended together in their works.

8. How is the macabre expressed in the work of the Rohan Master (fig. 745)?

9. In what way did altarpieces play a part in the development of Northern art?

10. Why did the Northern painters prefer oil to tempera surfaces?

11. Detail the story of Saint Bridget in the painting entitled *Nativity* by the Master of Flémalle, Robert Campin (fig. 746).

12. Explain the term *rising perspective* and how it was used by Campin.

13. Describe the complete interior setting for the *Mérode Altarpiece* (fig. 747).

14. Give the meaning for all the symbols in Joseph's carpentry shop in the *Mérode Altarpiece*.

15. What is meant by the statement, "Other naturalistic artists *represent* nature; van Eyck seems to *present* it"?

16. Sketch a brief biography of van Eyck's life.

17. Describe the atmospheric technique van Eyck used in the *Baptism of Christ* (fig. 749).

18. How was a sense of balance and unity achieved in the altarpiece at Saint Bavo's, Ghent (fig. 750)?

19. Locate the Gothic characteristics in the above-mentioned altarpiece.

20. What do you notice about the painting *Madonna of Chancellor Rolin* which would have been unheard of during the Middle Ages (fig. 754)?

21. How is a sense of perspective created in the above-mentioned painting? How is a sense of precision and microscopic detail achieved?

22. What is the theme of van Eyck's *Arnolfini Wedding* (fig. 756)?

23. Explain the symbolic meaning of the dog, the one lit candle, the hand on stomach, the statue of St. Margaret, the removal of shoes, and the convex mirror in *Arnolfini Wedding*.

24. How has Gothic *realism* and Renaissance *humanism* been joined in this loving couple?

25. Explain how van Eyck used light and darkness to create a stoic and controlled expression in his *Portrait of a Man in a Red Turban* (fig. 758).

26. What did the Italian humanist Bartolomeo Facio mean when he called van Eyck the "prince of painters of our age"?

27. In what way did Roger van der Weyden's paintings remain more Gothic in appearance than his master's?

28. State the theme of van der Weyden's *Deposition* (fig. 759).

29. Compare van der Weyden's *Deposition* with Grünewald's *Crucifixion*.

30. Describe how the technical and the expressive are joined in Bouts's *Last Supper* (fig. 761). State the theme.

31. Explain and state all the symbolism in van der Goes's *Portinari Altarpiece* (fig. 762). What makes it a joyful work?

32. How have the technical and the narrative come together in the works of Memlinc (figs. 764–767)?

33. Describe the significance of light in Geertgen Tot Sint Jans's *Nativity* (fig. 768).

34. What is the hallucinatory theme of Bosch's *The Garden of Earthly Delights* (fig. 771)?

35. Describe Eve. What does she symbolize for Bosch?

36. What is the meaning of the following in Bosch's work: a rat, owls, bear, the color blue, donkeys, and shells?

37. From his works, what is Bosch's position on sex?

38. Why do the figures appear more sad than happy?

39. Show how Bosch's hell is "manmade" as opposed to a typical medieval conception.

40. Relate how punishment fits the crime in Bosch's hell.

41. In the *Presentation in the Temple* (fig. 774) by Lochner, describe how a soft style was achieved. How does he treat size in this work?

42. Compare a work of Mantegna with one of Michael Pacher (fig. 776).

43. What impact did Schongauer's engravings (fig. 777) have on Michelangelo?

44. Describe the scene in Fouquet's *Marriage of the Virgin* (fig. 779).

45. What is so quintessentially French about Quarton's *Avignon Pietà* (fig. 780)?

CHAPTER FOUR

The High Renaissance In Central Italy

1. Outline the history of Italy from 1492 to 1503.

2. Why was Italy politically divided during the Renaissance?

3. Compare the two ideal men of the Renaissance, Alberti and Leonardo da Vinci.

4. What is the significance of knowing that Leonardo was left-handed?

5. Explain what Leonardo meant when he said that men were like "sacks of food"?

6. What are Leonardo's views on painting, music, and sculpture?

7. Explain the difference between planar and block architecture, and Leonardo's plans and perspective architecture.

8. How did Leonardo build up *chiaroscuro* in his *Adoration of the Magi* (fig. 785)?

9. Describe the scientific Leonardo in the mysterious grotto scene from *Virgin of the Rock* (fig. 786).

10. How do we know that this is a religious scene?

11. What guides our eyes to the center of the painting?

12. In the *Last Supper*, at what point did Leonardo choose to paint this dramatic event (fig. 789)?

13. Describe how Leonardo was able to capture the emotions and passionate responses of the twelve apostles.

14. Identify and explain symbolic symbols in this work.

15. Explain how his use of perspective in the *Last Supper* was different from what Leonardo had previously done.

16. Where and how is the nucleus created in the work *Battle of Anghiari* (fig. 788)?

17. What is the meaning of the painting *Madonna and St. Anne* (fig. 789)?

18. Give a brief historical background of the painting *Mona Lisa*, and state your opinion of that curious smile (fig. 790).

19. An historian called Leonardo "the most perceptive eye in an age of perception." Explain this statement.

20. Explain Michelangelo's position on painting and sculpture.

21. Michelangelo's destiny was to free the *imprisoned* sculpture from the stone. What did this statement mean, and how does it relate to his *Crossed-leg Slave* (fig. 791)?

22. State the theme of the *Pietà* (fig. 792).

23. What impact did Dante's statement, "Virgin Mother, daughter of thy Son," have on Michelangelo?

24. Who does Mary symbolize in the *Pietà*?

25. How does the colossus *David* symbolize the meaning of humanism and the city of Florence (fig. 793)?

26. Explain what Michelangelo meant when he said, "David with the sling, I with the bow."

27. Like Leonardo, describe the psychological moment Michelangelo chose to depict the *David.*

28. The last *tour de force* of Michelangelo was the statue *Moses*. Interpret this work as a depiction of cosmic cataclysm (fig. 794).

29. What does the term *contrapposto* mean, and how was it used in the *David* and the *Rebellious Slave* (fig. 796)?

30. Why is the Sistine Ceiling considered Michelangelo's greatest masterpiece and perhaps the most powerful painting in Western civilization (fig. 797)?

31. Highlight the chronology (order) of the Sistine Ceiling.

32. "In the beginning was the Word, and the Word was with God, and the Word was God." Describe this Word in the form of the Creator.

33. In the *Creation of Adam*, how is God the Father of man created in the image of Adam (fig. 799)?

34. Who is the most profoundly tragic figure in the Sistine Ceiling painting by Michelangelo, and why?

35. Describe all the classical elements in Bramante's Tempietto (fig. 800).

36. In what way did Leonardo have an impact on Bramante?

37. Explain what Carlo Dolci, a Florentine painter, meant when he said that "the greatest tragedy for painting was that Raphael died young, with a glorious reputation throughout Europe."

38. State the theme of Raphael's *The Marriage of the Virgin* (fig. 805).

39. Describe how a circular rhythm and perspective were maintained in *The Marriage of the Virgin*.

40. What is the symbolic meaning of the young man breaking his rod while Joseph's blossomed into a lily?

41. How did Raphael summarize the most significant idea of Renaissance humanism in his *School of Athens* (fig. 808)?

42. Describe how Raphael was able to express and summarize the most complex philosophical doctrines of Plato and Aristotle.

43. Identify as many as possible of the personalities in *The School of Athens*.

44. Compare Raphael's Renaissance madonna and child with any Byzantine painting of the same subject (fig. 806).

45. Explain the following point by Herman J. Wechsle in his book *Old Masters*: "[Raphael's madonnas] . . . have just enough of the earthly to make them desirable to man and just enough aloofness to reserve them a place in ethereal hierarchy."

46. Explain the meaning of Raphael's *Disputa* (fig. 807).

47. How does the Botticelli influence, the Hellenistic pose, and the Michelangelesque heroic come together in the *Gallatea* of Raphael (fig. 812)?

48. In what way is Raphael's *Transfiguration* different from the traditional rendering of the subject (fig. 813)?

In the following schematic drawings, state the architect and the work.

(1) _____

_____

(2)

_____

_____

(3)

_____

_____

(4)

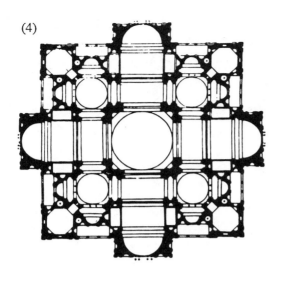

_____

_____

(5)

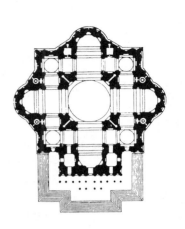

_____

_____

(6)

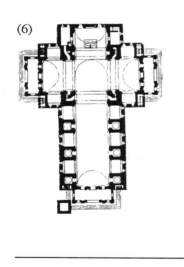

_____

_____

(7)

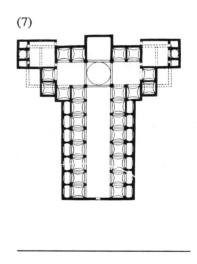

_____

_____

CHAPTER FIVE

Michelangelo And Mannerism

1. With the *Last Judgment* a new style of Western art was introduced that the Italians called *maniera*. Explain this term and style (fig. 818).

2. What caused this sudden and abrupt change from the classical idea of equilibrium to the anticlassical ideas of the neurotic and unstable in art?

3. In what way did mannerism have an influence on the next period in art, the Baroque?

4. For the Medici tombs, why did Michelangelo choose to idealize the two dukes in death (figs. 814, 815)?

5. State the theme of Night and Day according to the explanation given by Michelangelo.

6. Describe the style of mannerism in this tomb.

7. What is the symbolic meaning of the grinning mask and the owl?

8. Locate the anticlassical elements in Michelangelo's Entrance Hall in the Laurentian Library (fig. 817).

9. Based on Matthew 24:30–31, explain what makes the *Last Judgment* the most tragic and devastating interpretation of these words (fig. 818)?

10. In what way has Michelangelo depicted the awesome Christ in his *Last Judgment* as compared to his slender Christ in the *Pietà*?

11. Pietro Aretino was known as the "Scourge of Princes." Why did Michelangelo choose to paint him as St. Bartholomew (fig. 819)?

12. How did Michelangelo return to the dimensions of Bramante's plan for St. Peter's (figs. 820, 821)?

13. Why is the effect of Michelangelo's dome lost?

14. What did Michelangelo mean when he said about Brunelleschi's Dome of Santa Maria del Fiore: "I will make her sister dome. Larger, yes, but not more beautiful."

15. Describe Michelangelo's ideas as reflected in the Palazzo dei Senatori in Rome.

16. Why would modern artists appreciate Michelangelo's *Rondanini Pietà* (fig. 824) more than his earlier *Pietà*?

17. How did Andrea del Sarto, in his *Madonna of the Harpies*, remain faithful to the ideas and grace of the High Renaissance (fig. 825)?

18. Describe the characteristics of mannerism in del Sarto's work.

19. Recognize and define the mannerist style in Pontormo's *Deposition of Christ* (fig. 827).

20. Is there a focal point in this painting? Where does it begin? Where does it end?

21. What makes the *Deposition* an unrealistic scheme?

22. Explain what makes Fiorentino's *Descent from the Cross* so disturbing (fig. 828).

23. In the plasterlike painting, *Exposure of Luxury* by Bronzino, list and explain all the allegorical meanings contained in this work (fig. 839).

24. Describe how Caravaggio used chiaroscuro to create a dramatic effect in his painting *Holy Night* (fig. 830).

25. Explain how Caravaggio's *Assumption of the Virgin* conveys a sense of the supernatural (fig. 831).

26. In the *Jupiter and Io* painting, how have the human and divine come together (fig. 832)?

27. How has Parmigianino glorified the mannerist's love for distortion in his *Madonna with the Long Neck* (fig. 833)?

28. What makes this painting an enigma?

29. Write a short historical biography of Sofonisba Anguissola, one of the great female painters in Western art.

30. In what way is Michelangelo's influence apparent in the works of Cellini (fig. 836)?

31. In what way is Bologna's work different from that of Michelangelo's (fig. 837)?

32. Alberti defined beauty ". . . to be a harmony of all the parts . . . fitted together with such proportion and connection, that nothing could be added, diminished or altered, but for the worse." How is this statement reflected in the works of Vassari (fig. 838)?

33. Compare Ammanati's style of architecture (fig. 839) with that of Vassari.

34. By looking at the dramatic facade of the Church of the Gesu, how could one say that this edifice became the archetype for the Baroque style of architecture (fig. 841)?

CHAPTER SIX

The High And Late Renaissance In Venice

1. Venice, never a seat of learning, poured its wealth into what fields?

2. Why did Tuscan mannerism have only a slight influence on Venetian art?

3. Compare Giorgione's *Enthroned Madonna* (fig. 842) with Bellini's madonna.

4. What is the theme of the painting *The Tempest* (fig. 843)?

5. Describe the landscape in this painting.

6. How is color significant in the works of Titian?

7. Explain the meaning of the painting *Sacred and Profane Love* (fig. 844).

8. What is the symbolic meaning of a bowl partly filled with water and a plant bearing white roses in the aforementioned painting?

9. Compare Titian's *Assumption of the Virgin* (fig. 845) to Raphael's Sistine Madonna.

10. Describe the scene in Titian 's *Madonna of the House of Pesaro* (fig. 847).

11. How is a sense of balance achieved in Titian's *Man with the Glove* (fig. 848)?

12. What is your interpretation of the *Venus of Urbino* (fig. 849)?

13. What gives an indication that Titian's *Portrait of Pope Paul III and His Grandsons* is not a finished work (fig. 850)?

14. What is the meaning of Titian's *Rape of Europa* (fig. 851)?

15. Describe the movement and color in Titian's *Crowning with Thorns* (fig. 852).

16. How is Tintoretto's style of painting different from Titian's?

17. Why did the art critic John Ruskin accuse Tintoretto of "painting with a broom"? Give your assessment.

18. Retell the story of St. Mark freeing a Christian slave from the painting by the same name (fig. 814).

19. Describe Tintoretto's foreshortening in the aforementioned work.

20. What effect was Tintoretto trying to achieve in his *Crucifixion* (fig. 853)?

21. How did Tintoretto break with the traditional depiction of the Last Supper (fig. 855)?

22. What part do fire and light rays play in Tintoretto's *Last Supper*?

23. Compare the style of Veronese to that of Tintoretto.

24. What is so unusual about Veronese's painting of Christ in *Feast in the House of Levi* (fig. 856)?

25. Describe Veronese's color schematic for painting.

26. Explain the use of perspective in the *Triumph of Venice* (fig. 857).

27. In what way was Venice more suitable for the architect Sansovino than the city of Florence?

28. Describe how the Gothic, the Roman Doric, and the Egyptian obelisks come together to form a symphony of architecture in the Library of San Marco (fig. 858).

29. List the Roman characteristics in Palladio's Villa Rotondo (fig. 859).

30. Explain the statement that Palladio's architecture is "frozen music."

31. How did Palladio solve the problem of creating a high central pediment with lower sloping side-aile roofs (fig. 861)?

CHAPTER SEVEN

The High And Late Renaissance
Outside Italy

1. In what area were German artists deficient in comparison to Italians during the High Renaissance?

2. Explain how the Germans mastered the art of line in painting.

3. Explain how Dürer achieves his ideal conception of an artist in his *Self-Portrait* (fig. 862).

4. Why was Dürer called the "Master Engraver"?

5. What do the *Four Horsemen of the Apocalypse* represent (fig. 863)?

6. Explain the symbols in Dürer's *Adam and Eve* (fig. 864).

7. What is the meaning of his *Knight, Death, and the Devil* (fig. 865)?

8. How does Dürer idealize St. Jerome as the ideal contemplative of Christ and as a scholar (fig. 866)?

9. In Dürer's *Melancolia*, what does she represent? What do the tools represent (fig. 867)?

10. Describe the color, symbolism, and meaning of Dürer's *Adoration of the Trinity* (fig. 868).

11. State Dürer's position on Luther, the papacy, and Protestant extremists as it relates to his *Four Apostles* (fig. 869).

12. Describe how Grünewald's obsession with horror relates to the fact that his works contain all the agonies and triumphs of the human spirit.

13. State the theme of Grünewald's *Crucifixion* (fig. 870).

14. How has Grünewald brought out the human nature of Christ (fig. 871)?

15. The writing next to the arm of John the Baptist is from John 3:30, "He must increase, but I must decrease." Explain this in light of Grünewald's *Crucifixion*.

16. Describe the cycle in the painting *The Annunciation* (fig. 872).

17. What was Altdorfer's greatest gift as a painter and how is it expressed in the *Battle of Alexander and Darius on the Issus* (fig. 873)?

18. Compare this battle scene with those of Ucello and Leonardo.

19. In what way is Cranach's *Apollo and Diana* different from Italian classical models (fig. 874)?

20. Explain how Holbein the Younger is important to the history of art.

21. Describe the Leonardesque in Holbein's *Madonna of Burgomaster Meyer* (fig. 877).

22. How did Holbein display his virtuosity in the aforementioned painting?

23. Describe the quiet interior setting and point out the meticulous objects in Holbein's *The French Ambassadors* (fig. 875).

24. The "Defender of the Faith" is painted by Holbein as an absolute and independent monarch, not as a religious leader. Explain this statement (fig. 876).

25. Analyze and compare the portrait of Henry VIII by Holbein with that of Francis I by Clouet.

26. In what way is the *Apelles with Alexander the Great and Campaspe* more mannerist than Renaissance in style (fig. 879)?

27. How do the Gothic tradition and the native French style come together in the château of Chambord (fig. 880)?

28. Describe how climate played a role in the design of the Square Court at the Louvre. Describe the French character in this work (fig. 881).

29. What makes Goujon's Nymphs relief mannerist in style (fig. 882)?

30. How is emotionalism expressed in Pilon's *Deposition* (fig. 887)?

31. Explain what was original in Netherland's art in the early 16th century.

32. How does Gossaert render space and light in his *Agony in the Garden* (fig. 888)?

33. Describe the effect of landscape in Patinir's *St. Jerome* (fig. 889).

34. Explain why Pieter Bruegel is sometimes referred to as an "encyclopedic narrative painter" (fig. 891).

35. If the Italian Renaissance did not inspire Bruegel, what did?

36. Relate the story of Daedalus and how it is depicted in Bruegel's *Landscape with the Fall of Icarus* (fig. 890).

37. How does Bruegel handle the tragedy taking place in the above-mentioned work?

38. Describe the people, animals, and devastation in Bruegel's *The Triumph of Death* (fig. 891).

39. How has Bruegel captured the breathtaking winter landscape in his *Hunters in the Snow* (fig. 893)?

40. Explain what Carel Van Marder meant when he said that when Bruegel "crossed the Alps, he swallowed up all the mountains, and cliffs and spat them out again on canvas and panel. . . ."

41. Why are Bruegel's genre scenes important to the history of art?

42. How do people emerge from Bruegel's *Harvesters* (fig. 892)?

43. What part did religion play in destroying the culture and people of Latin America?

44. State the symbolic meaning of the Escorial (fig. 894).

45. El Greco, after viewing the Sistine Chapel, said, "Michelangelo was an extraordinary man and a great sculptor, but he had no idea of painting. He tried to carve figures in paint and he did not understand color." Explain this statement as it relates to the works of El Greco.

46. What is the theme of El Greco's *Burial of Count Orgaz* (fig. 896)?

47. Describe how the above-mentioned painting is divided into two parts.

48. What makes this vertical painting of the Count mannerist in style?

49. In the *Grand Inquisitor Don Fernando Nino de Guevara*, El Greco abandoned his distortion style. Explain and describe the result (fig. 898).

50. How is extreme emotionalism achieved in El Greco's *Resurrrection* (fig. 897)?

PART FOUR/The Renaissance

Match the artist with the work of art by inserting the proper number in the blank provided.

_____	*Feast in the House of Levi*	**1.** Giotto
_____	*The Burial of Count Orgaz*	**2.** Lorenzetti
_____	*Slaughter of the Innocents*	**3.** Masaccio
_____	The Escorial	**4.** Pisano
_____	*Hunters in the Snow*	**5.** Uccello
_____	*Melancolia I*	**6.** della Francesca
_____	Villa Rotonda	**7.** Botticelli
_____	*Crucifixion* of *Isenheim Altarpiece*	**8.** Michelozzo
_____	*French Ambassadors*	**9.** Brunelleschi
_____	*Habakkuk*	**10.** Donatello
_____	*Apollo and Diana*	**11.** Mantegna
_____	*Battle of Alexander and Darius*	**12.** da Messina
_____	*Rape of the Sabine Woman*	**13.** Limbourgs
_____	Dome, Cathedral of Florence	**14.** van Eyck
_____	*St. Mark Freeing a Christian Slave*	**15.** Bramante
_____	*August,* from *Tres Riches Heures*	**16.** Rossellino
_____	*Sacred and Profane Love*	**17.** Alberti
_____	*Arnolfini Wedding*	**18.** Ghiberti
_____	*The Tempest*	**19.** van der Weyden
_____	Palazzo Medici-Riccardi	**20.** Bosch
_____	*Madonna with the Long Neck*	**21.** Leonardo da Vinci
_____	*Jupiter and Io*	**22.** Sluter
_____	*Descent from the Cross*	**23.** Raphael
_____	Malatesta Temple, Rimini	**24.** Vasari
_____	Library of S. Marco	**25.** Verrochio
_____	*Exposure of Luxury*	**26.** Pontormo
_____	*Garden of Delights*	**27.** Bronzino
_____	*Entombment*	**28.** Correggio
_____	Facade, the Gesù	**29.** della Porta
_____	*Perseus and Medusa*	**30.** Parmigianino
_____	*David*	**31.** Giorgione
_____	*Madonna of the Rocks*	**32.** Titian

_____ *School of Athens*

_____ *Lamentation*

_____ *St. Jerome in His Study*

_____ *Equestrian Monument of*
           Bartolomeo Colleoni

_____ *Allegory of Good Government*

_____ *Dead Christ*

_____ *Primavera*

_____ *Story of Abraham*

_____ Tempietto, S. Pietro

_____ *Federigo da Montefeltro*

_____ *Tribute Money*

_____ Palazzo degli Uffizi

_____ *Battle of San Romano*

33. Tintoretto
34. Sansovino
35. Michelangelo

36. Veronese
37. Dürer
38. Grünewald
39. Cellini
40. Palladio
41. Cranach
42. Holbein
43. de Herrera
44. Bruegel
45. El Greco
46. Bologna
47. Altdorfer

Compare and contrast the following works of art.

Madonna Enthroned

Cimabue

Giotto

Annunciation

Martini

Broederlam

David

Donatello   Michelangelo

Last Supper

Castagno   Leonardo da Vinci   Bouts

Define the following terms and, if possible, state a work of art in which they appear.

chiaroscuro

Luzuria

Pietà

Mannerism

Disputa

In surto

Venus pudica

_____
_____

pietra serena

_____
_____

terra verde

_____
_____

tondo

_____
_____

palazzo

_____
_____

Divine proportion

_____
_____

predella

_____
_____

sinopia

_____
_____

gesso

_____
_____

tempera

_____
_____

Chronology: Distinguish between the Early, High, and Late Renaissance by indicating before each artist the period in which he was active. Use the letters E for Early Renaissance, H for High Renaissance, and L for Late Renaissance.

Bruegel _____

Michelangelo _____

Holbein _____

Jan van Eyck _____

Giorgione _____

Ghiberti _____

Dürer _____

Masaccio _____

Bellini _____

Raphael _____

Filippo Lippi _____

Grünewald _____

Bosch _____

Uccello _____

Leonardo _____

Botticelli _____

Prepare a GLOSSARY by citing the name of an artist that corresponds with the following descriptions.

GLOSSARY OF ARTISTS

_____ (1404–1472) An Italian architect who wrote treatises on painting (*Della pittura*) and architecture which helped spread the appreciation for classical Roman style.

_____ (1480–1513) German engraver and painter; follower of Dürer. Painted landscapes in a romantic vein.

_____ (1511–1592) Italian architect and sculptor who collaborated with Vignola and Vasari on Pope Julius III's villa. He designed the facade of Pitti Palace (Florence) for Cosimo de' Medici.

_____ (1430–1479) One of the first painters of Italy to utilize the Flemish technique of oil painting.

_____ (1426–1516) Was the Venetian teacher of Giorgione and Titian. His works are characterized by serenity, majesty, and luminous color.

_____ (1529–1608) Flemish sculptor whose real name was Jean Boulogne. His most famous works are *The Rape of the Sabines* and *Flying Mercury*.

_____ (1460–1516) Flemish painter who treated such themes as Paradise and the Last Judgment as fantasies; his characters take on diabolical characteristics. His *Garden of Earthly Delights* was bought by Philip II of Spain.

_____ (1444–1510) Florentine painter who mastered the art of color and rhythmic line.

_____ (1470–1478) Painter from the Netherlands, famous for the landscape backgrounds of his altarpiece panels.

_____ (1444–1514) Italian architect of the High Renaissance. His Cancelleria Palace and circular Tempietto in Rome reflect his love of classical antiquity.

_____ (1502–1572) Florentine painter whose real name was Agnolo Tori. He painted mostly portraits of celebrated figures such as Cosimo I de' Medici.

_____ (1525–1569) Father of Flemish genre and landscape painters; painted in vibrant colors the fields and forests of his native land. His peasants are robust at work and play, as in his painting *The Harvesters*.

_____ (1377–1446) Considered by many to be the first great architect of the Renaissance of Italy. His most famous works are the octagonal dome of the Cathedral of Florence and the Pazzi Chapel.

_____ (1375-1444) Flemish artist, identified with the Master of Flémalle. He was the teacher of Roger Van der Weyden.

_____ (1417–1457) Florentine master of realism; major works are the frescoes in Sant'Apollonia monastery in Florence.

_____ (1250–1330) Italian paintr and mosaicist who influenced Cimabue and Giotto.

_____ (1500–1571) Italian sculptor in metalwork who did the famous *Perseus with the Head of Medusa* in Florence.

_____ (c. 1302) Florentine painter and teacher of Giotto. He was the traditional artist from the Byzantine formal style to the more naturalistic Renaissance manner.

_____ (1494–1534) Italian Baroque painter whose real name was Antonio Allegri. Greatly influenced Italian painting during the 16th and 17th centuries by his use of foreshortening and the soft, moving contrast of color, light, and shade.

_____ (1472–1553) German artist whose real name was Sunder or Muller. He was a master of piquant line and silhouette in nudes, portraits, and religious paintings.

_____ (1452–1519) The supreme example of Renaissance genius in the form of artist and scientist.

_____ (1541–1604) Italian architect who completed some of the works of Michelangelo and Vignola, in such notable works as the Farnese Palace and the dome of St. Peter's.

_____ (1386–1466) Early Florentine sculptor of the Renaissance who abandoned the Gothic style for realism.

_____ (1471–1528) German artist famous for his prints and drawings through keen observation and rich detail. Most popular works are *Melencholia I*, *Knight, Death, and the Devil*, and *St. Jerome*.

_____ (1278–1319) Founder of the Sienese school of painting. The double altar in Siena's cathedral is the only authenticated work by him.

_____ (1541–1614) Born Domenikos Theotokopoulos in Crete, he studied in Rome and Venice and settled in Toledo, Spain. In his own time he was not very popular as an artist, but today he is considered by many critics as one of the greatest painters of all time. Vibrant colors and distorted and elongated figures are his trademark.

_____ (1390–1441) Flemish painter, who along with his brother Hubert, was the first to use resin or oil medium to create richness of color. His most famous painting is the *Arnolfini Wedding*.

_____ (1370–1427) First Italian painter to represent the Umbrian school of painting. Retained the Umbrian use of gilt ornament and glowing color.

_____ (1415–1480) Founder of the French school of painting during the Renaissance. Influenced by the van Eycks and early Florentines.

_____ (1387–1455) Florentine painter of religious subjects in the form of frescoes in the convent of St. Marks in Florence.

_____ (1378–1455) Florentine sculptor who won the competition in 1401 to carve the bronze doors of the Florence Baptistery. The subject of the doors deals with scenes from the Old Testament and the life of Christ.

_____ (1449–1494) Florentine painter who taught Michelangelo. His frescoes are famous for contemporary Renaissance portraits and settings.

_____ (1266–1337) Florentine artist who introduced naturalism in his painting through the use of expressive faces and movements.

_____ (c. 1440–1482) Flemish painter of realism and rich detail in his portraits and the Portinari altarpiece.

_____ (1480–1530) German religious painter, famous for his *Isenheim Altarpiece* in Colmar which portrays the passion of Christ with dramatic realism.

_____ (1497–1543) An outstanding German painter of the Renaissance. Made many portraits of eminent persons such as Erasmus and Henry VIII.

_____ (1245–1314) He assisted his father in creating the pulpit for Pisa's cathedral and the great fountain for Perugia. His masterpiece was the pulpit for Sant'Andrea.

_____ (1220–1287) Italian architect and sculptor who combined the elements of the Gothic and classical into his works. Best-known works are the marble pulpits for the cathedrals of Pisa and Siena.

_____ (1429–1492) Said to have been the first artist to study anatomy by dissection, he is famous for his drawings and paintings of muscular figures.

_____ (1494–1557) Florentine painter who imitated Michelangelo in such works as *The Visitation*, *Descent from the Cross*, and *The Holy Family*.

_____ (1374–1438) Italian sculptor who created the Gaia Fountain in Siena and the central doorway of San Petronio in Bologna.

_____ (1483–1520) Raffaello Sanzio (or Santi), considered one of the greatest artists in Western civilizaiton. His works are graceful, tender, and intellectual.

_____ (1400–1482) Florentine sculptor, famous for his enameled terra cotta.

_____ Antonio (1427–1479) was a Florentine sculptor, while Bernardo (1409–1464) was a Florentine architect who built the Rucellai Palace in Florence and sculpted the tomb of Lionardo Bruni in Santa Croce.

_____ (1455–1534) Italian architect who designed the Farnese Palace and the Pauline Chapel (Vatican).

_____ (1486–1531) Florentine painter famous for his frescoes and his oils. His work is marked by monumental composition and sumptuous color.

_____ (1445–1491) German engraver noted for his religious works. Among his most important works are *The Wise and Foolish Virgins* and *Adoration of the Magi.*

_____ (1428–1464) Florentine sculptor known for his church decorations and marble busts of children and women.

_____ (d. 1406) Netherlandish sculptor famous for realistic and powerful works at Dijon.

_____ (1406–1469) Florentine Carmelite priest who was a master of color and graceful line.

_____ (d. 1451) German painter of the Cologne school.

_____ Two Sienese painters who introduced naturalism into Sienese art.

_____ (1431–1506) Italian painter from the Paduan school of art. Strongly influenced by classical antiquity, he was a master of perspective and anatomy.

_____ (1401–1428) His real name was Tommaso di Ser Giovanni, born in Florence. Considered the pioneer of the Italian Renaissance through his use of perspective and naturalistic treatment of people and landscape.

_____ (1253–1344) From the Sienese school of painting, he was a master of delicate, sinuous line.

_____ (1430–1494) Flemish religious painter, follower of the van Eycks and Van der Weyden.

_____ (1475–1564) The greatest painter, sculptor, and architect of the Italian Renaissance. In his works there appears to be a unity of sculpture, painting, and architecture, especially in his painting of the Sistine Chapel.

_____ (1396–1472) Italian sculptor and architect who, along with Brunelleschi, shared leadership in establishing the Renaissance style. Built the Riccardi Palace and the Medici Chapel in Florence.

_____ (1518–1580) Italian architect of the late Renaissance whose most famous treatise is entitled *The Four Books of Architecture.*

_____ (1503–1540) Born Francesco Mazzolo in Parma, Italy, he was a Mannerist painter and is credited with introducing the technique of etching into Italy.

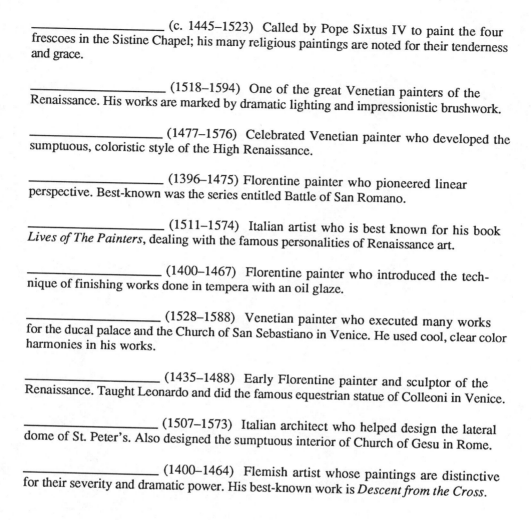

_____ (c. 1445–1523) Called by Pope Sixtus IV to paint the four frescoes in the Sistine Chapel; his many religious paintings are noted for their tenderness and grace.

_____ (1518–1594) One of the great Venetian painters of the Renaissance. His works are marked by dramatic lighting and impressionistic brushwork.

_____ (1477–1576) Celebrated Venetian painter who developed the sumptuous, coloristic style of the High Renaissance.

_____ (1396–1475) Florentine painter who pioneered linear perspective. Best-known was the series entitled Battle of San Romano.

_____ (1511–1574) Italian artist who is best known for his book _Lives of The Painters_, dealing with the famous personalities of Renaissance art.

_____ (1400–1467) Florentine painter who introduced the technique of finishing works done in tempera with an oil glaze.

_____ (1528–1588) Venetian painter who executed many works for the ducal palace and the Church of San Sebastiano in Venice. He used cool, clear color harmonies in his works.

_____ (1435–1488) Early Florentine painter and sculptor of the Renaissance. Taught Leonardo and did the famous equestrian statue of Colleoni in Venice.

_____ (1507–1573) Italian architect who helped design the lateral dome of St. Peter's. Also designed the sumptuous interior of Church of Gesu in Rome.

_____ (1400–1464) Flemish artist whose paintings are distinctive for their severity and dramatic power. His best-known work is _Descent from the Cross_.

PART FIVE

The Baroque

CHAPTER ONE

The Seventeenth Century In Italy

1. Baroque, "the art of the impossible," in Italian (*baroco*) meant any "contorted" idea that was an obstacle to logical reasoning. Explain this statement and relate it to art.

2. Why did critics of the 19th century use the word Baroque in a derogatory way?

3. What are the characteristics of the Baroque style as compared to the Renaissance?

4. The Carracci brothers became instrumental "in the formation of a new renaissance." Explain.

5. What illusionistic principles did the Carraccis introduce in the ceiling fresco of the Palazzo Farnese (fig. 900) as it relates to the complex explanation of the power of love?

6. What are the two novel differences in landscape painting introduced by Annibale Carracci's *Landscape with the Flight into Egypt*?

7. Describe the conservative elements in ceiling painting as expressed in the works of Reni (fig. 903), Domenichino (fig. 904), and Guercino (fig. 905).

8. In what ways did Caravaggio paint in a style that was the antithesis of the preceding generation of mannerists and academician painters?

9. In *The Calling of St. Matthew* (fig. 906), why were conventional people shocked with Caravaggio's revolutionary realism? Describe how one's eyes follow the movement of the painting through the use of light.

10. Caravaggio accomplished what no other artist could do during his lifetime: to paint light in such a way as to convey the feeling of mystery, drama, and strength in a painting. Explain this statement as it relates to *The Conversion of St. Paul*.

11. Describe how the use of chiaroscuro, in the same genre tradition of Caravaggio, is expressed in the works of Artemisia Gentileschi (fig. 908). What is the theme of this work as it relates to her personal life?

12. Why is the facade of Santa Susanna (fig. 909) by Maderno considered the first true Baroque facade in Rome? Describe its Baroque characteristics.

13. Why was the extension of the nave of St. Peter's a disaster for Bramante's and Michelangelo's dome?

14. How did Maderno bring the giant order of Bramante's interior for St. Peter's under Baroque requirements for width and height?

15. Bernini's genius as an artist lay in his ability to combine architecture, sculpture, and painting in order to play on the emotions of the viewer and subject matter. Write a theme on this statement.

16. Compare Bernini's *David* (fig. 912) with the naked and composed *David* by Michelangelo.

17. In *Apollo and Daphne*, explain the split-second climactic action taking place in the metamorphosis of Daphne.

18. Describe the dramatic embroidered columns in Bernini's Baldachin (fig. 914).

19. How has Bernini (fig. 915) caught the moment when St. Theresa wrote in her diary that "the pain was so great that I screamed aloud; but at the same time I felt such infinite sweetness that I wished the pain to last forever"?

20. Instead of using a rectangular or circular plan, how did Borromini break with tradition and create an alternate plan for church architecture? Use fig. 921 as an example.

21. How does the facade of San Carlo (fig. 920) prepare the viewer for the interior? Use terms such as *curve*, *convex*, and *concave* in your discussion.

22. In the interior of Sant 'Ivo (fig. 922), describe the sense of rhythm and movement, and the rocking effect on the viewer.

23. Describe the technique and the subject matter employed in the ceiling fresco entitled *The Triumph of the Barberini* (fig. 927) by Contona.

24. What effect was Baciccio trying to achieve in his works (fig. 928)? Use the term *illusion* in your discussion.

25. How is perspective achieved ultimately in the works of Pozzo (fig. 929)?

26. Describe the Byzantine, Renaissance, and Baroque characteristics in Longhena's Sta. Maria della Salute (figs. 930 and 931).

27. In the Guarini dome for the Church of the Holy Shroud (fig. 933), Baroque architecture in Italy reached its most complex stage. Discuss this statement by describing the dome's unusual ribs and the diminishing triangular pendentives.

CHAPTER TWO

The Seventeenth Century
In Catholic Europe Outside Italy

1. Like the Renaissance, Baroque was invented in Italy. But unlike the Renaissance, Baroque eventually embraced many countries of Western Europe, Catholic as well as Protestant. Write an essay explaining this statement by showing how many countries were allowed to develop their own genius in this art style.

2. Describe the influence that Caravaggio had on the French painter La Tour (see fig. 934), and the differences between the two.

3. Compare and contrast the peasant scene of the Le Nain brothers (fig. 935) with Bruegel's (fig. 892).

4. In what way is Nicolas Poussin the "embodiment of the Classical spirit"?

5. What is the subject of Poussin's *The Rape of the Sabines*? Describe the composition. Has Poussin caught the psychological reaction of the women? What makes the work heroic on one side and religious on the other?

6. Explain what is meant by the term *Hypolydian mode* as exemplified in figure 938 by Poussin.

7. What is the significance of the tiny figures in the works of Lorrain (figs. 939 and 940)?

8. Compare the "cool" and "controlled" style of Champaigne (fig. 942) with the Baroque magnificence of Rigaud (fig. 943).

9. What is the French contribution to 17th-century architecture as seen in the Château of Blois, the Château of Vaux-le-Vicomte, and the Louvre?

10. In the facade of the grandest royal palace in the world, Versailles (fig. 947), describe the French "grand manner" of palace architecture.

11. Louis XIV of France was called the "Sun King." How is this statement reflected in the interior of Versailles?

12. What makes the Hall of Mirrors at Versailles (fig. 950) "inhuman" in scale?

13. Describe the simple proportions, absence of curves, and intimacy of the Grand Trianon (fig. 953) as compared to the Palace of Versailles.

14. Describe the Roman traditions found in the Church of the Invalides (figs. 954–956).

15. In what ways are French sculptured tombs (fig. 958) different from Italian?

16. Describe the brutal realism in *Milo of Crotona* (fig. 959) by Puget. How did Michelangelo and Bernini influence Puget?

17. Write a short biography of Peter Paul Rubens.

18. Describe the characteristics of the High Renaissance and the climactic Baroque style in Rubens's *Raising of the Cross* (fig. 960).

19. Describe the mounting spiral movement of men, women, and landscape in *Rape of the Daughters of Leucippus*. Compare this to Rubens's "spiral in reverse" (fig. 962).

20. Briefly discuss the theme of the composition, *Henry IV Receiving the Portrait of Maria de' Medici.*

21. In the above composition, notice the smiling nudes and lush females. How has our perception of the ideal form of feminine beauty changed from Rubens's?

22. Instead of the traditional portrait of a monarch on horseback, how has Van Dyck chosen to portray King Charles I of England (fig. 966)? Describe how Charles is able to dominate the scene.

23. How is the style of Ribera a reflection of Caravaggio? Describe the realistic figures in strong light and shade as exemplified in *Martyrdom of Saint Bartholomew* (fig. 967).

24. Discuss the vigorous realism and fine use of subdued color in Zurbarán's *Vision of Saint Peter Nolasco*.

25. Pedro de Mena's works (fig. 967) are "startlingly real and direct." Explain this statement.

26. In his masterpiece, *Las Meninas* (fig. 970), how has Velázquez caught a moment frozen in time? How is the composition a painting within a painting? Describe how Velázquez perceives himself in this work.

CHAPTER THREE

The Seventeenth Century
In Protestant Countries

1. How did commerce play a part in the development of Flemish art?

2. How are Dutch paintings different in subject matter from Italian paintings?

3. On whom and in what way did Caravaggio have an influence on Dutch art?

4. Explain what is meant by the term "little masters."

5. Discuss and describe the horizon, people, and foreground in Van Goyen's *River Scene* (fig. 975).

6. Describe the space, people, animals, and landscape in *Avenue at Middelharnis* (fig. 976). In what way did Bernini influence these works?

7. In the *Linen Cupboard* (fig. 979), De Hooch "celebrates the harmony of the perfect bourgeois household." Explain this statement.

8. Compare and contrast the above work with Jan Steen's household (fig. 980).

9. Adriaen Brouwer's works (fig. 980) make a social comment. Explain this statement by describing one of his works.

10. Dutch still-life painting tantalizes the viewer in many ways. Describe and explain this statement after viewing the works of Heda (fig. 982).

11. In what ways are the works of Saenredam (fig. 983) more austere than those of his contemporaries?

12. The genius of comic portraiture was Frans Hals. Write a short biography of Hals with this theme in mind.

13. In the *Banquet of the Officers of the Saint George Guard Company*, how has Hals created "individual" portraits of each man?

14. Describe the use of a diagonal shadow and the sense of bravura style that makes the *Laughing Cavalier* Baroque. Describe the phenomenal aspect of this painting by noticing the decorated sleeve.

15. Hals was an artist who painted no religious pictures, no nudes, no histories of famous events, no mythologies, and no landscapes. Instead, he gave to art great examples of what Dutch people looked like in contemporary Holland of the 17th century. Write an essay on this statement after viewing figures 986 and 987.

16. Judith Leyster depicts a sensitive subject in *The Proposition*. Detail the subject matter and the technique she employed in painting this work.

17. Write a short biographical essay on Rembrandt by using the following quotation from one of his contemporaries, Kaerten Kretzer: "I will not try to depict your fame, O Rembrandt, with my pen. Everyone knows the honor which is yours when I merely mention your name."

18. In *The Anatomy Lesson of Dr. Tulp*, how has Rembrandt dramatized the scene? Describe how he painted the scholars as compared to the calm and confident Dr. Tulp.

19. What makes *The Night Watch* a tour de force?

20. In what way did Rubens and Caravaggio influence the works of Rembrandt (see fig. 990)?

21. Rembrandt was the only Protestant Baroque artist of serious religious painting. Explain this statement after viewing figures 994 and 995 and noticing that these works are not done in the heavy Baroque Italian style but instead in an austere Protestant style.

22. The greatest of the genre painters in Holland was the "Painter of Delft," Jan Vermeer. Write a short biographical essay about him with this statement in mind.

23. In the *Kitchen Maid*, how has Vermeer taken a mundane subject and made it a work of art? Compare his women with Rubens's heavy bundles of naked pink flesh.

24. In his *Allegory of Painting*, Vermeer painted his explanation of the purpose of art. What is it? Who is the female sitter? What is the symbolic meaning of the crown of laurel, the trumpet, and the volume by Thucydides? What is the meaning of the map in the background with its twenty ships? What two things make this painting typically Baroque?

25. Externally, Banqueting House by Inigo Jones is in the style of Michelangelo. Explain this statement in relation to the scale of Versailles. Why is it so carefully proportioned?

26. Wren created an intellectual complex in his greatest work: St. Paul's Cathedral (figs. 1003, 1004). How has he combined the elements of Classicism, the Renaissance, and Baroque into this one structure?

27. The dome of St. Paul's (fig. 1001) is one of the most perfect in the world. Explain why.

CHAPTER FOUR

The Eighteenth Century

1. Art in the 18th century took on a whimsical, fanciful, and lighthearted approach called the Rococo. Define and describe it.

2. Describe the use of landscape, space, mass, and structure in the works of Juvara (figs. 1005 and 1006).

3. As during the Renaissance, Venice poured its wealth into art during the 18th century. Explain this and give examples.

4. Lightness and grace are the hallmarks of the Venetian painter Piazzetta. Verify this statement by describing his *Ecstasy of St. Francis*. Compare it to Bernini's *Ecstasy of St. Theresa* (fig. 915).

5. Describe the technique employed by Tiepolo in his fresco paintings in order to cover large surfaces, as seen in figures 1008 and 1009.

6. Guardi's paintings are evocative, subjective, fanciful, somber, and lightful. How are these qualities shown in his works (fig. 1010)?

7. How is the Rococo an extension of the Baroque, but more delicate and lavish in its interior decoration?

8. Why is the Hôtel Soubise (fig. 1011) by Boffrand considered the *pièce de résistance* of French Rococo style? Describe the walls, ceiling, mirrors, windows, and gold leaf moldings in your discussion.

9. Describe how a modest-sized building, the Petit Trianon (fig. 1015), was erected on the same grounds at Versailles, but not in the "grand manner." Use terms such as *proportion*, *harmony*, *balance*, and *uniformity* in your discussion.

10. The French painter Watteau specialized in a transitory world of painting known as *fêtes galantes*. Explain the meaning of this.

11. Watteau's most celebrated masterpiece of Rococo painting is the *Pilgrimage to Cythera* (fig. 1017). Detail the subject matter of this lighthearted painting.

12. Boucher "more than any other [painter] epitomizes the pleasure-loving aspect of the Rococo. . . ." Explain.

13. In an era of artificiality and frivolity, there did emerge an observer of serene reality in 18th-century France, Jean Baptiste Chardin. Write an essay discussing his genre paintings of petite bourgeoisie subjects.

14. How is Chardin's *House of Cards* (fig. 1020) a typical Rococo scene, domestic but noble at the same time?

15. Greuze's works evoke a sentimental and moralizing message. Explain.

16. How is the joyous quality of the Rococo and the height of overfrivolous painting evident in the works of Fragonard?

17. In what way did Labille-Guiard invent a new way of posing for group portraits?

18. Vigée-Lebrun painted *Marie Antoinette and Her Children* (fig. 1025) as the queen wished to be remembered. Support this statement.

19. In what ways did Clodion parallel the works of Fragonard and Bernini?

20. French Classical architecture of the 1700's was not exportable, while Germany and Austria adopted Rome's elastic Baroque and Rococo styles because they were elastic. Explain this statement.

21. The facade of the majestic, throned Monastery of Melk by Jakob Prandtauer illustrates one of the most important characteristics of the Rococo. What is it? In your discussion use terms such as *line*, *movement*, *convex*, and *concave*.

22. Describe the exterior of the undulating facade of the Pilgrimage Church of Vierzehnheiligen (fig. 1031) by Neumann.

23. The Vierzehnheiligen interior is a masterpiece. Describe it by discussing the island altar, interlocking bays, and ceiling.

24. Baroque and Rococo art were not limited to religious objects. Indeed, what made Baroque and Rococo "popular" art was that they could be found in homes and princely palaces. Explain and give examples by describing the works of Neumann (fig. 1030) and Poppelmann (fig. 1033).

25. Write an essay on the following theme: the Renaissance did not make an impact on English architecture. No churches, villas, or chateaux were built in the Renaissance style since Queen Elizabeth was not a great patron of the arts. It was not until the Stuart reign that English architecture began to equal and perhaps surpass that of continental Europe.

26. In what way are foreign elements noticeable in the design of Radcliffe Library (fig. 1037) by James Gibbs?

27. Describe the Palladian features in Chiswick House (fig. 1038) by Burlington.

28. Give examples of what helped bring a revival of Gothic style into 18th-century England.

29. Satiric wit and narrative candor are the hallmarks of the English painter Hogarth. Describe one of his works in detail.

30. "Beauty of his color and the delicacy of his touch" are the characteristics of Thomas Gainsborough. How is this concept reflected in his *Mary Countess Howe* (fig. 1045)?

31. The artificial and unnatural are evident in the works of Reynolds. Explain this statement after viewing *Lady Sarah Bunbury Sacrificing to the Graces* (fig. 1042).

32. Write a short biographical essay and describe the style of Angelica Kauffmann.

33. John Singleton Copley, an American, is remembered for his solid portraits of Yankee merchants. In his portrait of *Paul Revere*, describe this painting as it relates to the above-stated theme.

34. In what way was the American painter Benjamin West a forerunner of Romanticism?

PART FIVE/The Eighteenth Century

Chronology: After each date listed below, write the name of the person or event associated with it.

1715–74 _____

1726 _____

1737 _____

1740–48 _____

1742–45 _____

1756–63 _____

1762 _____

1774 _____

1776 _____

PART FIVE/The Baroque

Match the artist with the work of art by inserting the proper number in the blank provided.

_____ *Calling of St. Matthew*	1. West
_____ *Aurora*	2. Houdon
_____ *Apollo and Daphne*	3. Copley
_____ *Judith with the Head of Holofernes*	4. Neumann
_____ Sant'Agnese, Rome	5. Watteau
_____ Chapel of the Holy Shroud	6. Prandtauer
_____ *Raising of the Cross*	7. Gibbs
_____ *Madonna of the Rosary*	8. Gainsborough
_____ *Triumph of Bacchus*	9. Juvara
_____ *Vision of St. Peter Nolasco*	10. Gabriel
_____ *Newborn*	11. Chardin
_____ *The Cart*	12. Boffrand
_____ Vaux-le-Vicomte	13. Fragonard
_____ Louvre	14. Wren
_____ Banqueting House	15. Caravaggio
_____ *The Night Watch*	16. Rubens
_____ *River Scene*	17. Hals
_____ *Kitchen Maid*	18. Reni
_____ *The World Upside Down*	19. van Dyck
_____ St. Paul's Cathedral	20. Jones
_____ *A Pilgrimage to Cythera*	21. Bernini
_____ Superga Church	22. Velázquez
_____ Hôtel de Soubise	23. Rembrandt
_____ *Copper Cistern*	24. Gentileschi
_____ Petit Trianon	25. Zurbarán
_____ *The Bathers*	26. Vermeer
_____ *Voltaire*	27. Borromini
_____ Abbey, Melk	28. Perrault
_____ Residenz, Wurzburg	29. Guarini
_____ Radcliffe Library	30. Le Vau
_____ *Mary Countess Howe*	31. Louis Le Nain
_____ *Paul Revere*	32. La Tour
_____ *Death of General Wolfe*	33. van Goyen
	34. Steen

205

PART FIVE/Baroque Art

Prepare a GLOSSARY from the list below by citing one name for each statement.

GLOSSARY

Gabriel / Gibbs / Houdon / Borromini / Baldacchino / Bernini / Hals / Guarini / Fragonard / Boffrand / Caravaggio / Chardin / Fischer / Neumann / Watteau / Vignola / della Porta / Prandtauer / Vermeer / Rembrandt / Rococo / Rubens / Velázquez / van Dyck / Tiepolo

_____ Founder of the Society of Jesus.

_____ German Baroque architect who is most noted for his churches and the Palace of Würzburg.

_____ Italian architect who, with the help of Vignola, completed the dome of St. Peter's

_____ Austrian architect whose most famous work is the Monastery at Melk in Austria.

_____ A great Dutch painter and etcher from Leiden who worked in Amsterdam most of his life.

_____ A style of art that made use of such forms as shells, scrolls, and flowers during the 18th century.

_____ Foremost Flemish painter who produced over 2000 works of art, mostly for the Spanish and French courts.

_____ Venetian painter from Italy who painted frescoes in churches and palaces.

_____ Flemish painter of portraits and religious scenes.

_____ Court painter for Philip IV of Spain. His most notable painting is _Las Meninas_ (_The Ladies-in-Waiting_).

_____ Dutch painter who produced fewer than forty works of art. His scenes are of intimate interiors with solitary women.

_____ Italian architect who designed the lateral dome of St. Peter's. He also designed the sumptuous interior of the Gesù in Rome.

_____ Painter of sensuous, gay scenes of open-air festivities.

206

_____ French architect who designed the Petit Trianon at Versailles.

_____ English architect whose finest work is St. Martin's-in-the-Fields.

_____ French sculptor whose works include *George Washington* and *Voltaire.*

_____ A marble structure built in the form of a canopy over the altar of a church.

_____ One of the greatest Italian sculptors and architects of the Baroque style. Carved the graceful statue of *St. Theresa* and designed the elliptical colonnades of St. Peter's.

_____ Italian painter who mastered the dramatic effect of light and shade.

_____ One of the great French genre painters of still lifes and domestic interiors.

_____ One of the nine Greek goddesses of arts and sciences who was also the muse of history.

_____ Austrian architect, notable for his Karlskirche.

_____ French painter of love and gallantry for the aristocracy.

_____ Dutch painter of single and group portraits. His themes dealt with the common life.

PART SIX

The Modern World

CHAPTER ONE

Neoclassicism

1. Neoclassicism was a reaction against the artificiality, pomp, and emotionalism of the Baroque and Rococo. Explain this statement by using terms such as *reason*, *objectivity*, and *moderation*.

2. What major problems may result from an art, such as Neoclassicism, that is based on imitation and total acceptance of academic standards and laws?

3. Give examples of how Neoclassicism became an international style for "official" government art and academia.

4. Describe the Neoclassic elements in Jefferson's home at Monticello (fig. 1051) and the University of Virginia (fig. 1052).

5. Latrobe's Catholic Cathedral of Baltimore is in the Neoclassical style. Describe its characteristics.

6. In what way did Neoclassicism fail in the interior of the Church of the Madeleine (fig. 1056)?

7. The leading exponent of Neoclassicism in France was Jacques-Louis David. His works dealt with history, allegory, and mythology. Write a short biographical essay with this statement in mind.

8. How is David's ardent republicanism evident in his *Oath of the Horatii*? What is the subject and theme of this work?

9. In what ways are Michelangelo's *Pietà* and Caravaggio's light incorporated into David's *Death of Marat* (fig. 1060)?

10. Instead of a scene from antiquity, Ingres painted a work entitled *The Valpinçon Bather* (fig. 1062). This is his idea of feminine beauty, not in the face, but in the "lost profile." Explain this remark.

11. Houdon is considered one of the greatest portrait sculptors in history. How has he depicted the frail Voltaire as a universal and timeless individual?

12. By far the most famous work of Canova was his *Maria Paolina Borghese, as Venus Victrix* (fig. 1068). How has Canova presented the sister of Napoleon in the style of David and Ingres?

CHAPTER TWO

Romanticism

1. Romanticism was a reaction against the Enlightenment. Instead of *Cogito ergo sum*—"I think, therefore I am"—it became "I feel, therefore I am." Write an essay on this theme.

2. In what ways did the artist's conception of himself change during the Romantic period as compared to previous ages? Use the term *bohemian* in your discussion.

3. Humanitarianism and socialism are themes common in Romantic art. Explain and give examples of works expressing these ideas.

4. The mystique of nature, with its aura of mystery and sense of foreboding, had what profound influence upon the Romantic artist?

5. Discuss the following statement: Romanticism produced an art that was an "elevation of emotion above intellect, content above form, color above line, intuition and passion above judgement, resulting in an entirely new ideal hero—Byron's Childe Harold and Goethe's Werther."

6. In the *Family of Charles IV* by Goya, how did he depict the royal family of Spain, especially the ill-natured queen and her pompous husband? Who is the only one in the group that stands out favorably?

7. As Goya began to lose his hearing and become desperately ill, he abandoned his early Rococo style and became a Romantic artist. Write a short essay on how Goya's illness affected his works.

8. The first artist to comment on a shocking contemporary event was Goya. Explain.

9. Instead of glorifying war, how has Goya shown us the physical and psychological horrors of war, of man's inhumanity to man?

10. Discuss the focal point ("the rebel") in Goya's *Third of May*.

11. *The sleep of reason produces monsters* is Goya's most important etching from *Los Caprichos*. Explain the meaning of this work as we see the artist asleep at his drawing desk, surrounded by monsters and demons.

12. What is meant by the term "pious lies," in the works of Gros?

13. Describe the story that brought tens of thousands of people flocking to see a shocking and horrid episode in French naval history, the wreck of the government frigate *Medusa*, as depicted in Gericault's work (fig. 1078). How has he caught the dramatic moment when the survivors first sighted their rescue ship?

14. Write a short biographical essay on the best-known French Romantic, Eugène Delacroix. In your discussion use words such as *exotic*, *anti-academia*, and *history*, and describe Delacroix's love for the writings of Scott and Byron.

15. Describe how Delacroix has captured the holocaust of the pathos of defenseless women in his first great painting, *The Massacre of Chios* (fig. 1081).

16. In his *Woman of Algiers*, Delacroix has allowed us to visit a harem. Elaborate on this statement.

17. Compare and contrast the works of Rude (fig. 1085) and Carpeaux (fig. 1086) in their style of sculpture.

18. Why was Romanticism in painting, like Goethe in literature and Beethoven in music, accepted wholeheartedly in Germany?

19. In what sense are the works of Friedrich pantheistic? Use terms such as *solitude*, *mystery*, and *alienation* in your discussion.

20. What is the subject matter of Blake's *Circle of the Lustful*? Describe it.

21. Write a short biographical essay about the first major English Romantic landscape painter, John Constable. As your theme, use the following quotation by him: "For all painting is nothing else but feeling."

22. In what ways did Constable abandon the artificial "ideal landscape" of Neoclassicism in favor of a more "naturalistic" style (see figs. 1089 and 1090)?

23. Why did critics of the 19th century condemn the works of Turner as "unfinished"?

24. Constable praised Turner's works as "airy visions, painted with tinted steam." How is this statement true as it relates to Turner's *Rain, Steam, and Speed*? How is this painting a foreshadowing of Impressionism?

25. "The architecture of the Romantic movement is often of uncertain and irregular quality, yet it can be extremely successful in its picturesque. . . ." Write a theme on this statement; give examples.

CHAPTER THREE

Realism

1. Explain what "reality" meant for the Realist artist by using the term *objective* as opposed to *subjective*.

2. The Realist wanted to imitate nature without romanticizing it. Explain.

3. Explain the meaning of the following quotation by the Realist painter Courbet: "To know in order to be able to create, that was my idea. To be in a position to translate the customs, the ideas, the appearances of my epoch, according to my own estimation; to be not only a painter, but a man as well; in short, to create living art—this is my goal."

4. Explain what the Realists meant when they repudiated "ideal art" for the "actual." Use the following quotation by Courbet as your guide: "Show me an angel and I will paint one."

5. Write a short history of the early beginnings of photography.

6. How did daguerreotypes influence the development of painting?

7. Explain the term Calotype and compare it to daguerreotypes.

8. What interested Corot about Italian artistic tradition?

9. Explain what is meant by "the buildings and bridges of Rome were to [Corot] cubes bounded by planes, revealed by delicate changes of hue and value."

10. Describe how Corot suppressed architectural detail for a more softened effect in his painting *Chartres Cathedral* (fig. 1103).

11. How did the artist Millet capture the dignity and worth of the working-class peasant (fig. 1103)?

12. The purpose of Realism was not to portray something with photographic accuracy, but instead to record the contemporary "facts of life." How is this evident in the works of Daumier?

13. Detail the historical background for the painting by Daumier entitled *Rue Transnonain* (fig. 1104). How are the "facts" presented in this painting?

14. How has Daumier painted his *Third Class Carriage* in a manner reminiscent of Michelangelo's style?

15. *The Stone Breakers* by Courbet became synonymous with the proletariat and socialism. Explain why.

16. In *A Burial at Ornans* we have a recording of a rude and ugly fact of life. What makes the work Realistic? Courbet jokingly called the painting, "The Burial of Romanticism." Explain what he meant.

17. Describe the technique employed by Rosa Bonheur in her *Plowing in Nivernais* (fig. 1110).

18. Describe how the use of cast iron was incorporated to produce a pictorial architecture similar to Pompeii as exemplified in Labrouste's Reading Room, Bibliothèque Ste-Geneviève, Paris (fig. 1111), and Paxton's Crystal Palace (fig.1112).

19. In what ways did Corot and Courbet influence the works of Winslow Homer? Give examples.

20. Compare and contrast the *Gross Clinic* (fig. 1114) by the American painter Eakins with Rembrandt's *Anatomy Lesson of Dr. Tulp* (fig. 989).

21. Explain the meaning and purpose of the Pre-Raphaelites.

22. Describe in detail the characteristics and meaning of the Pre-Raphaelite paintings entitled *The Carpenter's Shop* (fig. 1115) by Mallais and *The Last of England* by Ford Madox Brown.

CHAPTER FOUR

Impressionism—
The Art of Pure Vision

1. The first of the "modern" movements in the history of art took place with an exhibition entitled "Société Anonyme des Artistes Peintres." It was held in Paris in April 1874. Write a short history of this show and the controversy surrounding it.

2. Romanticism, the last tour de force, was over and a new look at nature (*plein air*) had begun. Explain.

3. The new subject matter for the Impressionist would be what Zola called "a slice of life." Write a short theme on this statement as it relates to art.

4. What did the Impressionist want to capture at a glance with no detail?

5. Explain how the Impressionist wanted to catch the "play of light" on the surface of an object as opposed to the traditional chiaroscuro method.

6. *Impression—Sunrise* (fig. 1117), by Monet, is the work that gave its name to the movement. Describe what makes this painting a mystery, an illusion.

7. Write a short biography on Edouard Manet, the forerunner of Impressionism and modern art.

8. *Luncheon on the Grass* by Manet created an uproar and shocked visitors who saw it. Why? Describe the scene. Is there a meaning?

9. Describe the snapshot effect of Manet's *Execution of the Emperor Maximilian* (fig. 1119). Compare it to Goya's *Third of May* (fig. 1072).

10. Write a short essay on the following theme: Monet's goal was to capture the "temporary moment" on canvas through the use of light and color.

11. Monet's *Women in the Garden* (fig. 1120) shows the importance of painting directly outdoors. Describe this genre of painting with this statement in mind.

12. By studying figures 1121 and 1122, describe how Monet's figures are "spots" of color, entirely without contour and lines.

13. What result was Monet trying to achieve in his works *Water Lilies*? Use terms such as *mystical*, *abstract*, and *form* in your discussion.

14. In the *Folies-Bergère* (fig. 1123) by Manet, how is the influence of Velázquez evident?

15. Write a short biography of the great female Impressionist painter, Berthe Morisot.

16. Characterize the distinctive style of lightness and transparency, delicacy, and tranquility in Morisot's *The Dining Room* (fig. 1125).

17. Explain what Cézanne meant when he said so eloquently, "Perhaps we all came from Pissarro."

18. Use the following quotation by Pissarro to describe his *Boulevard des Italiens, Paris* (fig. 1126): "I am delighted to paint Paris streets that are generally considered ugly though they are so silvery, sparkling and full of life."

19. Explain what Renoir meant when he said that *color* and *volume* were equal if not superior to the concept of "light" as advocated by the Impressionist.

20. Renoir once remarked, "The world knew how to laugh in those days! Machinery had not absorbed all of life: you had leisure for enjoyment and no one was the worse for it." With this quotation in mind, how has Renoir caught those days in his *Moulin de la Galette* (fig. 1127)? Who are the individuals and what is the theme of this work?

21. What were some of the favorite themes of Degas?

22. How does Degas capture, define, draft, and redraft the portraits of his dancers?

23. The female nude—close up, in an awkward position, at her bath—was a favorite subject for Degas. Explain in detail the meaning of this statement with help from the following quotation by Degas: ". . . the nude has always been represented in poses which presupposed an audience, but these women of mine are honest, simple folk, unconcerned by any other interests than those involved in their physical condition."

24. In what ways was Rodin similar to and different from the Impressionist because of his medium?

25. At the Salon of 1877, Rodin exhibited a nude male figure (fig. 1133) for which he was praised by some, while others accused him of having "cast from a living figure." Explain why.

26. What impressed Rodin about the technique of Michelangelo and how did he incorporate it into his works, especially in *The Kiss* (fig. 1134) and the *Gates of Hell* (fig. 1135)?

27. What are the themes of Rodin's *Burghers of Calais* (fig. 1136) and *Balzac* (fig. 1137)?

28. Explain how Impressionism was not only a revolution involving style, light, and color, but how it also enabled women to begin proliferating the arts as never before.

29. Write a short biography of the expatriate female artist, Mary Cassatt, who said, "I am American. Simply and frankly American."

30. Cassatt's paintings, pastels, and drawings have a charm about them without ever being sentimental. Explain this after viewing figure 1140.

31. What was novel about the pose in Sargent's work entitled *Portrait of Lady Agnew*?

32. Describe the effect Saint-Gaudens was trying to achieve in his *Monument to Admiral Farragut* (fig. 1142).

CHAPTER FIVE

Post-Impressionism—
A Deeper Reality

1. What does the term *Post-Impressionism* mean? What was it a reaction against? Use terms such as *line*, *structure*, *solidity*, *stability*, *volume*, and *weight* in your discussion.

2. Explain what Cézanne meant when he said that he wanted "to make Impressionism something as solid and durable as the old masters in the museums." Use terms such as *cubes*, *cylinders*, and *pyramids* in your discussion.

3. Discuss the following idea: the Post-Impressionists were "expressionist" rather than "impressionist."

4. One of the most enduring appeals of Post-Impressionism is the sharply individual style of each artist, something that was very difficult to distinguish among the Impressionists at times. Write a short theme on this statement using the following quotation: ". . . each Post-Impressionist artist created a sharply individual style, which could no longer be mistaken for that of any of his contemporaries or former associates, in subject matter, content or technique."

5. Why is Cézanne called the "Father of Modern Art"? Use terms such as *nonrepresentative*, *volume*, and *solidity* in your discussion.

6. How did Impressionism have an impact on Cézanne and what did he want to do with it? Use the following quotation by Cézanne as your guide: "I do not hide it, I too have been an Impressionist. Pissarro had enormous influence on me. But I wanted to make Impressionism solid and lasting like the art in museums."

7. Describe the theme of Cézanne's landscape entitled *Mont Sainte-Victoire* (fig. 1143) by using the following quotation by him: "Painting from nature is not copying the object, it is realizing one's sensation." In your discussion, note the sequences of planes and colors.

8. How is Cézanne's still life (fig. 1144) different from 17th-century Dutch still-life painting? Is there a symbolic or religious meaning? Explain the pictorial distortion of Cézanne's perspective in this work.

9. Cézanne's most popular paintings are sequences dealing with card players (fig. 1145). Are there any psychological character references about his players? Use terms such as *static*, *rustic*, and *solid* in your discussion.

10. In the *Great Bathers* (fig. 1147) by Cézanne, why did critics scorn this strange work? How are the nudes painted? How do nature and man come together in this work?

11. Seurat had one objective in art, and that was to make the "fleeting" moment of Impressionism "timeless." Explain this by describing the technique of pointillism.

12. *Sunday Afternoon on the Island of La Grande Jatte* (fig. 1149) by Seurat is his most controversial work. Why? Describe the silhouette figures.

13. Why did Lautrec decide to enlarge his work, *Moulin Rouge*?

14. Write a short biography of Gauguin before he became a full-time painter.

15. Gauguin escaped from the Western civilization of horse races, theaters, cafes, and industrial society to the unspoiled and primitive "tropical paradise." Explain.

16. How do the "imaginative" and "real" come together in Gauguin's *Vision After the Sermon* (fig. 1152)?

17. Gauguin's *The Day of the God* (fig. 1156) brought about fin de siècle and the beginning of a new era of modern art. Explain what is meant by this statement by using the words of Gauguin: "If my works do not survive there will remain the memory of an artist who liberated painting from many of its former academic defects. . . . Criticize me if you wish for having failed, but not for having tried."

18. Elaborate and give examples of what Van Gogh meant when he said: "Instead of trying to reproduce exactly what I have before my eyes, I use color more arbitrarily so as to express myself forcibly."

19. Van Gogh believed in the expressive power and symbolic meaning of color to create emotional effects. Explain.

20. In Van Gogh's *View of La Crau*, the painting "reads" like a story. "Read" this painting by describing the story contained in it.

21. Van Gogh judged his painting *The Night Café at Arles* as "one of the ugliest pictures I have done." Yet this provincial town pool hall contains all the human conditions associated with that room. What are they?

22. Interpret Van Gogh's *Starry Night* with these words by the artist: "[I had] a terrible need of—shall I say the word?—of religion. Then I go out at night to paint the stars. . . ."

23. Explain the meaning of *symbolism* as applied to art. Use the works of Redon in your discussion.

24. What was the meaning and purpose of a group of artists know as the Nabis? Use the works of Vuillard (fig. 1158) as your guide.

25. James Ensor was more interested in emotional expression than in style, color, or form. Explain.

26. In *The Sleeping Gypsy* by Rousseau, what new style is being introduced?

CHAPTER SIX

The Fauves And Expressionism

1. The term *Fauves*, meaning "wild beasts," was coined by the French critic Vauxcelles. What does this term mean in the context that it was used at the Paris Salon d'Automne of 1905? Characterize this style of art.

2. Why did the painting by Matisse entitled *The Green Stripe* (fig. 1165) particularly outrage critics?

3. What is the theme of Matisse's *Joie de Vivre* (fig. 1163)? Use the terms *bacchanal, arcadian, color,* and *landscape* in your discussion.

4. Explain how Matisse's *Red Studio* is a summation of his art and philosophy by observing the individually painted objects.

5. Describe the oriental background, the profusion of objects, and the complexity of the pose in Matisse's *Decorative Figure Against an Ornamental Background*.

6. Explain why Matisse decided not to include color in the murals at the Chapel of the Rosary of the Dominican Nuns in Vence, France.

7. How are the prostitutes in the works of Rouault (fig. 1169) portrayed quite differently from Lautrec's?

8. How did Gothic tracery of irregular pieces of glass influence the work of Rouault (fig. 1170)?

9. Tolstoy implied that an artist "communicates emotion" by "inflicting" the emotional attitudes portrayed in his works on his viewer. Explain this statement as it relates to the term *Expressionism*.

10. Kaethe Kollwitz was a woman painter with strong social convictions. How is this statement evident in her work *Outbreak* (fig. 1171)?

11. Why is Paula Modersohn Becker significant for contemporary art?

12. The Die Brücke regarded themselves as a revolutionary group in art. How is this statement true as seen in the grotesque characterization of such a traditional Christian theme as the *Doubting Thomas* (fig. 1173) by Nolde?

13. The Blaue Reiter was more interested in freedom of experimentation than Die Brücke's revolutionary attitude toward social protest. Explain.

14. Marc's animal paintings (fig. 1174) contained constructed shaped lines as well as color for symbolic rather than naturalistic reasons. Explain.

15. Describe the apocalyptic theme in Kandinsky's *Improvisation 30* (fig. 1175).

16. In what way is the work *Composition 234: Bright Circle* (fig. 1176) a pioneer painting in the field of abstract art?

17. What is the allegorical meaning of Kokoschka's *The Bride of the Wind* (fig. 1177)?

18. Beckmann's experiences in the First World War are clearly seen in his *The Night*. Describe the brutality of this work by concentrating on the physical as well as the psychological mutilation of images.

CHAPTER SEVEN

The Search For Form—
Cubism And Abstract Art

1. In what way is Maillol considered the transitional sculptor from the fluid Impressionism of Rodin to the more modern works of art? Use his *Mediterranean* sculpture (fig. 1181) as your guide.

2. Explain how Expressionistic elongation is the key to understanding the style of Lehmbruck (figs. 1182, 1183).

3. The reality of life was more important to Picasso than art or nature. How is this evident in his "Blue Period" (fig. 1184)? Use terms such as *dense blue palette* and *pessimism* in your discussion.

4. In Picasso's "Rose Period" his palette lightened toward pinks and grays. Describe how these colors created the passive mood and theme for his *Family of Saltimbanques*.

5. Describe why *Les Demoiselles d'Avignon* (fig. 1186) is considered the summation of Picasso's early works and the beginning of a revolutionary new phase known as Cubism.

6. How did African tribal art inspire Picasso? Give examples.

7. What is meant by the term *Analytical Cubism* as exemplified in the works of Braque (fig.1188) and Picasso (fig. 1189)?

8. What is meant by the term *Synthetic Cubism*? Use the term *collage* in your discussion.

9. Who are the men in Picasso's *Three Musicians* (fig. 1191)?

10. How is the classical flavor evident in Picasso's *Three Women at the Spring* (fig. 1192)?

11. Detail the historical subject background of the great *Guernica*. Why is it considered by many critics to be Picasso's masterpiece?

12. In what ways is Leger's Cubism significantly different from Picasso's and Braque's?

13. "Color Cubism" may be one way to describe the works of Delaunay. Explain this statement by describing his *Homage to Bleriot*.

14. How was Duchamp able to depict movement of the body in motion as seen in his *Nude Descending a Staircase* (fig. 1196)?

15. In what ways are traces of African sculpture noted in the works of Brancusi (fig. 1197)?

16. In *Bird in Space* (fig. 1189), Brancusi has eliminated details while retaining the characteristics of the species. Explain.

17. Animal energy and mechanistic forms are found in Raymond Duchamp-Villon's *Horse* (fig. 1199). Explain this blending.

18. Describe in a Cubist manner how the human figure is treated in Archipenko's *Walking Woman* (fig. 1200).

19. How are Lipchitz's relief works of still lifes (fig. 1201) reminiscent of Cubist paintings?

20. Although Italy stood as a symbol for the past in art, it was the birthplace of Futurism. Explain this statement by showing how the Futurists disclaimed the classical past by glorifying youth, speed, danger, energy, and destruction.

21. How is a sense of dynamism conveyed by Boccioni in his *The City Rises*?

22. How does Boccioni convey the essence of movement in his polished bronze *Unique Forms of Continuity in Space* (fig. 1205)?

23. Joseph Stella described the Brooklyn Bridge as "the shrine containing all the efforts of the new civilization *America*." Explain this by examining his romanticized image of industrial New York in his *Brooklyn Bridge*.

24. What was the aim of Rayonnism as exemplified in figure 1207?

25. Explain how *The Knife Grinder* (fig. 1208) by Malevich contains elements of Cubist fragmentation and Futurist multiplication of images.

26. Is there any representational logic in Malevich's *Suprematist Composition* (fig. 1209)?

27. Describe the architectonic characteristics of the paintings by Popova (fig. 1210).

28. What was the symbolic and functional intention of Tatlin's *Monument to the Third International* (fig. 1211)?

29. Explain the term Constructionism as it applies to the creation of three-dimensional abstracts. Use the works of Gabo (fig. 1212) as your guide.

30. Concave and convex surfaces create what sensation in the works of Pevsner (fig. 1213)?

31. How are art and architecture linked together in the painting *Proun 99* (fig. 1214) by Lissizky?

32. The creed of De Stijl was utter simplicity. Explain this statement by using the terms *rectangles* and *colors* in your discussion.

33. Mondrian's representation of natural appearances became a pattern of verticals, horizontals, and occasional arcs. How are these characteristics represented in his works (figs. 1215, 1216)?

34. Describe the abstract relief work of Nicholson (fig. 1217) as a token of his tribute to Mondrian.

CHAPTER EIGHT

Fantastic Art, Dada, And Surrealism

1. "Everywhere the soul of man is in chains," claimed the Surrealist Manifesto in 1924. Explain this statement as it relates to Surrealist Art by discussing the *other reality*—unconscious, dreams, fantasies, and imaginings.

2. Individual fantasy and his love for his homeland are evident in Chagall's *Self-Portrait with Seven Figures* (fig. 1218). Explain this statement by describing this work.

3. Use the following quotation by Paul Klee to explain the meaning of one of his works (figs. 1220, 1221, and 1222): "Art does not reproduce the visible, but makes visible."

4. How did the senseless barbarities of World War I have an impact on the Dada movement? Try to explain its meaning by using the following quotation by the Dadaist, Tristan Tzara: "[Dada] was a state of mind."

5. Characterize the style of painting by Ary (figs. 1223, 1224), using terms such as *simplified, abstract, unbroken contours, movement,* and *lightness.*

6. Discuss the mixed media, the possible symbolic meaning, and provocative gesture of Duchamp's *Bride Stripped of Her Bachelors, Even* (fig. 1225).

7. Imagery of the bizarre and irregular perspective are seen in the works of Ernst (fig. 1227). Explain.

8. How did Schwitters free art from traditional materials and techniques?

9. Explain the *frottage* technique developed by Ernst. What impression did he create as a result of this technique in his apocalyptic *Europe after the Rain II*?

10. In what ways did Miró remain true to the basic Surrealistic principles?

11. Describe how fantasy, irrationality, imagination, and dreams are pronounced in Miró's *The Harlequin's Carnival*.

12. Describe the illusionism, hallucinatory luminosity, the neurotic sexual fantasies and fears in the paintings of Dali (figs. 1232, 1233).

13. How are the works (fig. 1235) of the Surrealist painter Magritte unlike those of his contemporary Dali?

14. Describe the surrealism in the works of Matta (fig. 1234) by using such terms as *humanoid and amoeba-like forms*, *cataclysmic encounter*, and *cosmic forces*.

CHAPTER NINE

American Art Of The Twentieth Century And Recent Movements Elsewhere

1. Write a brief history of the 1913 New York Armory Show and its impact on modern art.

2. Describe the Expressionist overtones of color and the military decorations in Hartley's *Iron Cross* (fig. 1237).

3. Use the following quotation from John Marian to describe the Cubistic and Futuristic elements in his work *Lower Manhattan*: ". . . the whole city is alive, buildings, people, all are alive; and the more they move me, the more I feel them to be alive. It is this moving of me that I try to express."

4. The works of O'Keeffe are not entirely based on abstraction but on closely observed natural appearances. Explain this by viewing her *Blue and Green Music* (fig. 1241).

5. Use the following quotation by Edward Hopper to explain the theme of loneliness and desolation in his work (fig. 1239): "I [don't] see it as particularly lonely. . . . Unconsciously, probably, I was painting the loneliness of a large city."

6. How did Davis arrange his works (figs. 1240, 1242) to suggest the environment of American life?

7. In what way is Mexican history interwoven with Marxism?

8. Use the following quotation by Orozco to explain the theme of his works (fig. 1243) and that of Siqueiros's (fig. 1244): "The mural is [the] highest, the most logical, the purest and the strongest form of painting."

9. From whom did early American Abstract Expressionists draw support and inspiration for their work?

10. How did Gorky fuse Surrealism with biomorphic abstraction in his work *Golden Brown Painting* (fig. 1245)?

11. Describe the "drip and splash" style for which Pollock (fig. 1246) is best known. Use the term *action painting* in your discussion.

12. Using the colors black and white and a system of planes and contours, what effect did De Kooning achieve in his painting *Excavation* (fig. 1247)?

13. Characterize the growing intensity of execution and expressionism in De Kooning's *The Time of the Fire* (fig. 1248).

14. Describe the distinctive style of Hofmann (fig. 1249) by using the following words: *squares*, *mass*, *unmodulated pigment*, and *space*.

15. How are the works of Klein (fig. 1250) reminiscent of Oriental calligraphy?

16. Use the following quotation by Mark Rothko to interpret his works (fig. 1251): "I paint large pictures because I want to create a state of intimacy. A large picture is an immediate transaction; it takes you into it."

17. What caused the reaction against Abstract Expressionism in the late 1950's and early 1960's?

18. Try to characterize Pop Art by using words such as *mass media*, *mass production*, *advertising*, and *the comics*.

19. Describe the method employed by Rauschenberg of combining commonplace objects, photographic silk-screen prints, and oil paint to produce works of art.

20 Jasper Johns's best-known paintings are of targets and the American flag. With the use of encaustic paint and unexpected elements (face masks), how do his works (fig. 1253) take on a disturbing meaning?

21. How does Lichtenstein imitate the screened images of comic strips to produce a painting such as *Whaam* (fig. 1254)? Does this work have a social comment to make?

22. Oldenburg's works may be described as "Soft Art." Explain this by viewing his *Soft Typewriter* (fig. 1255). What is the theme of this work?

23. From what sources did Andy Warhol take his subject matter?

24. What do the figures and groups of unpainted plaster casts by Segal (fig. 1257) capture about modern man?

25. What is meant by the term *packaging art* as exemplified in the works of Christo (fig. 1258)?

26. Describe the mixed media employed by Samaras to produce a work of art. Also, explain his experiment with light and reflection as seen in *Room No. 2* (fig. 1259).

27. How does Op Art differ from Pop Art? Use the works of Anuszkiewicz (fig. 1260) as an example.

28. Compare and contrast the art known as *color field* and *hard edge* by using the works of Kelly (fig. 1264) and Stella (figs. 1265 and 1266) as your guide.

29. In the paintings of Newman (fig. 1261), describe the monochromatic color fields.

30. Describe in detail the technique of painting employed by Louis (fig. 1262).

31. How are the paintings of Noland (fig. 1263) different from those of Louis in terms of size, color, complexity, and control?

32. Nevelson's sculpture may be characterized as "sculptural wall." Explain this by using words such as *boxes*, *pigeonholes*, *abstract*, and *ordinary objects*.

33. Use the term *constructive sculpture* to describe and explain the meaning of Bontecou's *Untitled* (fig. 1269).

34. Explain the term *minimal art* by using the works of Judd (fig. 1273) and Hesse (fig. 1270) as examples.

35. Explain and give examples of what is meant by *light sculpture* and *earth art.*

36. Photorealism is the art of transplanting the impression of a photographic image onto a flat canvas. Describe how this technique was applied by the artist Estes in his work *Downtown* (fig. 1275).

37. What is the meaning of Hanson's dreadful *Tourists* (fig. 1276) and Arbus's *Child with Toy Grenade* (fig. 1277)?

38. What is meant by the term "rough" or "raw" art? Use the works of Dubuffet (fig. 1280) as an example.

39. Describe and characterize the works of De Staet (fig. 1281) and Klein (fig. 1282).

40. What are the aims of Moore and Hepworth in their sculptural works (figs. 1283 and 1284)?

41. Characterize the work known as *In The Bay of Naples* (fig. 1285) by Hodgkin.

CHAPTER TEN

Modern Architecture

1. What impact did the "mechanized industrial complex" of the mid-19th century have on architecture?

2. What faults are noticeable in the use of cast iron as a building material? What is the advantage of using reinforced concrete with steel?

3. Richardson's Marshall Field Warehouse (fig. 1286) may be characterized in one work—utilitarian. Explain.

4. As a result of the use of the steel frame, what happened to the arch and the vault in 20th-century architecture?

5. In what ways did construction (metal frame) determine the form of the building in the works of Sullivan (fig. 1287 and 1288)?

6. Write a short essay characterizing the movement known as Art Nouveau.

7. How does the Church of Sagrada Familia (fig. 1289) by Gaudí seem to say "Good-bye to the past, hello to the future"?

8. Gaudí's Casa Mila (fig. 1290) has been characterized by some critics as "quarry" achitecture. Explain.

9. Describe how glass and iron are combined to decorate the Salon Van Eetvelde (fig. 1292) by Horta.

10. What part did reinforced concrete play in the work of Berg (fig. 1293)?

11. Describe the strong element of expressionism in the sweeping curved design of Mendelson's Einstein Tower (fig. 1294).

12. Describe what is meant by the ground-hugging "prairie" style of Frank Lloyd Wright (fig. 1296).

13. Explain how a dramatic setting, natural materials, and 20th-century construction techniques are blended together in Wright's Kaufmann House (fig. 1297).

14. Briefly describe the International Style that ignored national boundaries.

15. Describe how the Bauhaus is a symbol of 20th-century *rational* architecture.

16. How does open space penetrate the works of Le Corbusier (figs. 1301 and 1302)?

17. Use Mies's famous dictum, "Less is more," to describe his German Pavilion (fig. 1303) at the Barcelona International Exposition in 1929.

18. Describe how the Woolworth Building (fig. 1304) proved that the skyscraper could be beautiful.

19. How does the Chrysler Building (fig. 1305) reflect the fashion of its times, the 1930's?

20. Explain the innovative design introduced by Hood and Howells in their Daily News Building (fig. 1306).

21. The Lake Shore Apartments by Mies are masterpieces of aesthetic engineering. Explain.

22. How was the glass-curtain vertical wall of the Lever House offset by the long horizontal of the lower base?

23. What is the intent of the Post-Modern architects as exemplified in the works of Jahn (fig. 1310)?

24. The pilgrimage church of Notre-Dame-du-Haut, Ronchamp, was Le Corbusier's postwar masterpiece. Explain this statement by describing the material used and the external and irregular shape of the building to suit the needs of the modern-day worshiper.

25. How was Nervi able to vault large areas with dazzling effect?

26. How does Saarinen link the aestheticism of flight to the needs of passengers in his aerodynamic terminal for Dulles Airport (fig. 1315)?

27. Describe the impressions the following museum buildings have on the viewer from *without* and *within* in their sculptured forms: Whitney (figs. 1316 and 1317), Pompidou Center (fig. 1318), and Kimbell (fig. 1319).

28. Describe the freedom from uniformity for multiple housing in the works of Safdie (fig. 1320).

29. What part does color play in the architecture of Graves (fig. 1323)?

30. Describe the exterior of Meier's The Atheneum (fig. 1324) in relation to "the spirit of Le Corbusier."

31. How does Bofill's low-cost housing unit (fig. 1325) achieve a variety of effects on the viewer?

PART SIX/The Modern World

Match the artist with the work of art by inserting the proper number in the blank provided.

_____	*Oath of the Horatii*	1.	Canova
_____	*Los Caprichos*	2.	Géricault
_____	*Maria Paolina Borghese*	3.	Delacroix
_____	*Valpinçon Bather*	4.	Daumier
_____	*Abbey Graveyard Under Snow*	5.	Millet
_____	*Raft of the Medusa*	6.	Eakins
_____	*The Hay Wain*	7.	Manet
_____	*Massacre at Chios*	8.	Goya
_____	*Rue Transnonain*	9.	Monet
_____	*The Stone Breakers*	10.	Pissarro
_____	*Sower*	11.	Degas
_____	*The Gross Clinic*	12.	Morisot
_____	*Luncheon on the Grass*	13.	Seurat
_____	*Impression—Sunrise, Le Havre*	14.	Ingres
_____	*Nocturne*	15.	Cézanne
_____	*The Rehearsal*	16.	van Gogh
_____	*The Age of Bronze*	17.	Cassatt
_____	*In the Dining Room*	18.	Munch
_____	*The Bath*	19.	Corot
_____	*Boulevard des Italiens*	20.	David
_____	*Bathers at Asnières*	21.	Whistler
_____	*Mont Sainte-Victoire*	22.	Rodin
_____	*Vision After the Sermon*	23.	Friedrich
_____	*The Starry Night*	24.	Constable
_____	*The Scream*	25.	Courbet
_____	*Chartres Cathedral*	26.	Gauguin

PART SIX/Nineteenth Century

Chronology: In the list below, cross out the entries that do not belong under the period.

1780–1789
U.S. Constitution adopted
Pissarro, *Boulevard des Italiens*
Critique of Pure Reason by Kant
Roentgen discovers X-rays
David, *Death of Marat*

1800–1850
Napoleon crowns himself emperor
Communist Manifesto by Marx and Engels
Delacroix, *Death of Sardanapalus*
Houdon, *George Washington*
Edison invents motion pictures

1850–1900
Manet, *Luncheon on the Grass*
Ingres, *Valpinçon Bather*
Eakins, *The Gross Clinic*
Munch, *The Scream*
Crimean War
Unification of Italy
Cassatt, *The Bath*

PART SIX/Twentieth Century

Chronology: In the list below, cite the correct date for each entry.

Sigmund Freud publishes *Interpretation of Dreams* _____

Einstein formulates theory of relativity _____

Revolution in China _____

First Futurist Show _____

Armory Show, New York _____

Bauhaus founded _____

Mussolini seizes Italian government _____

First Surrealist manifesto _____

Spanish Civil War _____

Penicillin discovered _____

John Cage composes *Imaginary Landscape No. 4* _____

John F. Kennedy assassinated _____

First manned landing on the moon _____

Vietnam War ends _____

Buckminster Fuller publishes *Synergetics* _____

Ronald Reagan elected president _____

PART SIX/Chapters Six, Seven, Eight, and Nine

Complete the chart by describing the style and characteristics of each movement.

	Artist	Style	Characteristics
E X P R E S S I O N I S M			
C U B I S M			
F U T U R I S M			
F A U V E S			
D A D A			

	Artist	Style	Characteristics
S U R R E A L I S M			
A B S T R A C T E X P R E S S I O N I S M			
P O P A R T			

	Artist	Style	Characteristics
O P A R T			
M I N I M A L A R T			
E A R T H A R T			

Prepare a GLOSSARY from the list below by citing one name for each statement.

GLOSSARY

Millet / Winckelmann / Poussin / Turner / Cézanne / Gauguin / Fry / Seurat / van Gogh / Canova / Jones / Constable / Courbet / Ingres / Goya / Géricault / Daumier / Delacroix / David / Friedrich / Cassatt / Degas / Sisley / Renoir / Pissarro / Morisot / Monet / Manet

_____ Italian sculptor during the Neoclassical period. His most famous statues are of Napoleon and his family.

_____ English painter, noted for his landscapes, who worked directly from nature. His *Hay Wain* is one of his most notable works.

_____ French painter of the Realist school of art who was anti-authority in aesthetics and politics.

_____ French lithographer, sculptor, and painter who satirized bourgeois society.

_____ French painter who was an ardent republican by nature despite his work for Louis XVI and Napoleon.

_____ French Romantic painter who used bright colors and dynamic themes in his works.

_____ German Romantic painter of landscapes who declared that "the painter should paint not only what he sees in front of him, but also what he sees within him."

_____ He introduced Romanticism into France with his *Raft of the Medusa.*

_____ Spanish painter to the court of Charles III. Famous for his satirical etchings entitled *Los Caprichos.*

_____ (1780–1867) French painter who was an excellent draftsman and portraitist.

_____ English architect who brought the Neoclassical style to England.

_____ French realist painter; noted for his paintings of working-class peasants.

_____ (1594–1665) Leading French neoclassical painter; noted for his discipline in his works.

_____ (1775–1851) One of the greatest English landscape painters during the Romantic period.

_____ French Post-Impressionist painter who greatly influenced the course of modern art by his distortion of natural forms. His most important works deal with still lifes and landscapes of his native Provence.

_____ An English art critic who helped introduce the Post-Impressionist movement into England.

_____ French painter of the Post-Impressionist group who gave up his family and banking career for art. He went to Tahiti, where he painted his greatest works.

_____ Developed the pointillist technique of painting. His master-piece is the *Un Dimanche à la Grande Jatte.*

_____ Dutch Post-Impressionist painter; noted for the brilliant use of color in his landscapes, still-lifes, and portraits.

_____ An American painter and etcher who spent most of her artistic life in France.

_____ French Impressionist painter who worked in oils and pastels. Most of his work included ballet dancers and women at their baths.

_____ Never officially claimed as an Impressionist, he did influence them by capturing the fleeting moment in his works.

_____ He organized the first exhibition of the Impressionists in 1875, after the title of one of his paintings: *Impression—Sunrise.*

_____ Leading French female Impressionist. Typical of her works are scenes dealing with women at their bath, such as *La Toilette.*

_____ French Impressionist painter noted for his street scenes of Paris and London.

_____ French painter who began as an Impressionist but then abandoned that style after 1890. He was noted for his pictures of children, young women, and nudes.

_____ Born in Paris of English parents, he became an Impressionist painter famous for his landscapes.

Complete the chart by describing the style and characteristics of each architect.

	Style	Characteristics
R I C H A R D S O N		
S U L L I V A N		
G A U D I		
H O R T A		

	Style	Characteristics
W R I G H T		
G R O P I U S		
C O R B U S I E R		
R O H E		

	Style	Characteristics
G I L B E R T		
S K I D M O R E		
J A H N		
N E R V I		

	Style	Characteristics
B R E U E R		
P I A N O		
K A H N		
S A F D I E		

	Style	Characteristics
G R A V E S		
M E I E R		
B O F I L L		